PLAYING THE LONG GAME

How to Save the West from Short-Termism

Laurie Fitzjohn-Sykes

SOCIETAS
essays in political
& cultural criticism

imprint-academic.com

Copyright © Laurie Fitzjohn-Sykes, 2015

The moral rights of the author have been asserted.
No part of this publication may be reproduced in any form
without permission, except for the quotation of brief passages
in criticism and discussion.

Published in the UK by
Imprint Academic, PO Box 200, Exeter EX5 5YX, UK

Distributed in the USA by
Ingram Book Company,
One Ingram Blvd., La Vergne, TN 37086, USA

ISBN 9781845408343

A CIP catalogue record for this book is available from the
British Library and US Library of Congress

Contents

Introduction	1
Chapter One: The Problem of Short-Termism	4
Chapter Two: Why Companies Exist	18
Chapter Three: Ownership and Control	31
Chapter Four: Rise of Short-Termism	47
Chapter Five: What are the Alternatives?	61
Chapter Six: Reforming Incentives	81
Chapter Seven: The Missing Piece	94
Chapter Eight: Conclusion	112

Introduction

On the 25th June in 2010, Masayoshi Son, a Japanese businessman, gave a two-hour speech to the shareholders of Softbank for which he is CEO and a major shareholder. The speech was to lay out the company's business plan. As you can imagine, these presentations are not often that exciting. When attending the trick is to sit near the back and have a heavy dose of the free coffee, but this one was a little different. In addition to the shareholders, there were a thousand fans who had won tickets. The business plan being presented was not how to reach the targeted profit in a year's time. It was instead a 30-year business plan and a 300-year vision for the future. The speech touched on artificial intelligence, 200-year life expectancy and the development of telepathy.

You are probably thinking that this was delivered by some sort of bombastic CEO proclaiming to know the future. But Masayoshi Son comes across as a relatively unimposing figure. When he speaks you can sense the enjoyment he gains from what he does, there is a playfulness you rarely find in business leaders. If most CEOs gave such a speech, they would be met with ridicule. It is hard to know what will happen in a few years let alone 30 or even 300 years. And yet this speech was no great surprise to the audience, for Masayoshi Son has made his name by taking a long-term view, in a country already known for taking a long-term view. An attribute he would argue has helped him rise from humble beginnings to become the richest man in Japan.

Around the same time, I was accompanying the chief financial officer (CFO) of a major European company on some meetings to see existing and potential investors. The CFO's aim was to keep existing shareholders happy and persuade new ones to buy shares. Most investors would ask the same questions, to which management would give the same answers. Why had growth slowed? Would it improve next quarter? Why were profit margins not increasing as expected? Why were they investing in an area that would take years to deliver any benefit? Why was more money not being returned to shareholders via bigger dividends?

The difference between the two is stark, in one a CEO announces a 30-year plan to raptures of applause, in the other management is pressured for why the quarterly results were not better and why more cash is not being returned to shareholders. This shows the difference that can exist between how companies are run and what decisions they take. How some companies focus on the next 10 years, while others focus on the next quarter.

In the West, and especially the US and UK, businesses are increasingly focused on next quarter's profits in order to justify ever increasing executive compensation, with investment falling as a result. This is badly damaging our economy and accentuating the West's decline versus the East. I believe this is the most important issue of our time. We only succeed by investing and currently our businesses are not doing this. This book looks at how we got to this point and what we can do about it.

In the next chapter I outline the evidence for and costs of short-termism. Chapter 2 explains why and how companies developed. Chapter 3 looks at how the ownership and control of our companies has changed over the last hundred years, moving from families to financial markets. In Chapter 4 I explain how this has led to a short-term focus. In Chapter 5 I briefly explain some of the other models for company ownership around the world. Chapter 6 looks at some reforms to tackle short-termism, focusing on incentives. Chapter 7 then looks at the missing piece in the short-termism puzzle which is the information behind decisions.

Chapter One

The Problem of Short-Termism

> *"There is no quality in human nature, which causes more fatal errors in our conduct, than that which leads us to prefer whatever is present to the distant and remote."*
> —David Hume (*A Treatise on Human Nature*, 1740)

In the West we obsess about what our governments are doing; should they spend more on health, education or defence? How much immigration should they allow? In contrast, when it comes to business we assume they follow a set course determined by the pursuit of profit. We only worry whether profits are too high or how much the executives are being paid. We rarely ask, are they investing enough and in the right areas? The truth is that companies make some of the most important decisions in our economy.

Over the last hundred and fifty years companies have grown to dominate our economies. The majority of us who are not working for the government, work for a company. Companies have been behind all the major waves of innovation from railways to aeroplanes to the internet. The decisions our companies make are arguably more important than those made by our politicians. In general politicians argue about how to spend money, while companies make the decisions that determine if our economy will grow and in what direction.

Our public debate wrongly assumes that companies blindly follow profit along one path. In reality companies have a wide range of choices and discretion on what to do. They must provide something customers want, but this still leaves a large number of options. Importantly, these decisions all involve a balance between the short- and long-run. Does a company invest money in developing a new product that will take a few years, or increase the advertising spend on existing products with an immediate benefit? Does a company fire staff in a recession to protect profit margins, or retain the staff so that when the economy recovers it will still have sufficient expertise? Does a company invest or return cash to its shareholders?

There is a growing concern that companies in the West are increasingly making decisions that increase short-term profit to the detriment of their long-term success. As a result, investment is falling across Western economies. This is particularly worrying as it is hard to think of something that provides our current high standard of living that is not the result of long-term investment. We have to invest in infrastructure such as roads, railways and energy production. New technologies and medical advances are only achieved by allocating resources to research. Businesses only grow by investing, either to develop new products, increase manufacturing capacity or to break into new markets. And lastly, we only create more productive workers by spending on training and education. Without investment our businesses and hence our economy suffers.

The problem of short-termism in business is becoming more widely acknowledged, and the focus rightly falls on listed companies. These are the companies whose shares are bought and sold on the stock market rather than being privately owned. They are generally the largest companies in our economy, coordinating a significant proportion of our activity and carrying out the bulk of investment. They also support a much larger network of smaller companies such as suppliers, distributors and outsourcers. They are often the coordinating hub at the centre of an industry network.

Listed companies are important across the West, but more so in the UK and US. Of the 1,000 largest companies in the UK, 43% are listed compared to 17% in Germany, 19% in France and 11% in Italy.[1] In the UK there are around 1,300 listed companies. They employ 3.7m people, 16% of private sector employment and account for around 47% of UK domestic investment.[2]

Listed companies are also where the problem of short-termism is most acute. The concern is that the short-term focus of financial markets in turn pressures companies to act for the short-term. Daily trading of shares combined with management pay based on short-term share price performance creates a vicious cycle of mutually reinforcing short-termism. The focus of listed companies

---

[1] Franks, Mayer, Volpin and Wagner (2009) "The Life Cycle of Family Ownership: A Comparative Study of France, Germany, Italy and the UK".

[2] Pattani, A. and Vera, G. (2011) "Going Public: UK Companies' Use of Capital Markets", Bank of England Quarterly Bulletin 4: 322.

on meeting quarterly profit expectations has led to what many people call "quarterly capitalism".

I saw this short-term pressure repeatedly while working as an equity analyst. I would write research on companies' performance and valuation, advising investors when to buy and sell. I saw a number of companies that for a period were seen as golden examples of how to run a company, profit rising each quarter, returning cash to shareholders and the CEOs held up as heroes. However, in many occasions it turned out the company had been underinvesting and cutting costs too aggressively. Management had favoured short-term profit over the long-term health of the company. After the lauded CEO left, a painful crash would follow and the slow process of rebuilding the company would ensue.

Another aspect that shows the dangers of this short-term focus is recurring corporate scandals. These are nothing new, there have been corporate scandals since the first companies were formed hundreds of years ago. However, the occurrence seems to be increasing, Enron, Worldcom, Polly Peck, Lehman Brothers, Northern Rock, Madoff, Parmalat, LIBOR rates, FX rates and sub-prime mortgages are just some examples from the last few decades.

The specifics of each scandal and crisis differ, but behind each one was generally a desire to increase profits and the share price in the short-term. This drove executives at Enron to fraudulently push debt off the balance sheet, making the company appear successful until it eventually went bankrupt. Short-term incentives encouraged bankers to take on excessive long-term risk in pursuit of short-term profit in the lead up to the 2007/8 financial crisis. Or similarly the BP Deepwater Horizon oil spill is alleged to have been partly caused by reduced safety checks in order to save costs short-term.

In some companies and industries a short-term focus eventually leads to disaster. Such scandals and crises naturally capture our attention. However, this is not the most damaging impact of short-termism. For in the majority of companies short-termism does not lead to a crisis it just leads to consistently bad decisions, namely a lack of investment. Underinvestment in 99% of companies is far more problematic than the crises in 1%, the recent financial crisis being an exception.

The lack of investment is apparent across most Western economies, and this in turn is accelerating the West's relative decline versus the East. Fixed capital investment has been falling in most Western countries since the 1970s, as shown in Figure 1. The euro area is currently investing 18% of GDP, down from around 28% in the 1970s. The UK is at 15%, down from around 21% in the 1970s. The USA is investing 19%, down from around 24% in the 1970s. In contrast China is investing just below 50% of its GDP, up from around 35% in the 1970s. South Korea is investing around 28% of its GDP, broadly the same as the 1970s.

Before any economists reading this cry foul, part of the gap in investment rates can be explained as follows. Western economies have shifted away from capital intensive manufacturing towards services. Developing countries are also catching up and so have a naturally higher investment rate. They need to build the roads, buildings and power stations that we already have in the

West. However, these factors struggle to explain the whole gap, it is still worrying and a clear sign something is wrong with our system.

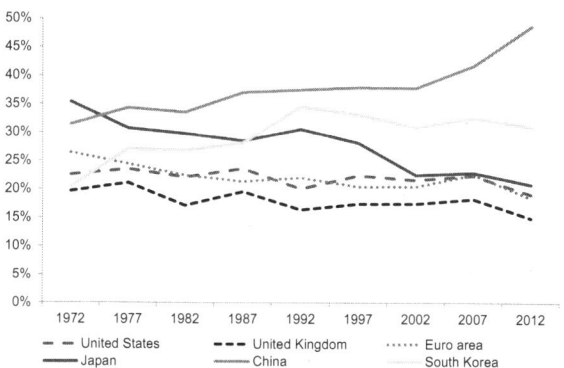

Figure 1. Gross fixed capital formation as a percentage of GDP. Source: World Bank Statistics.

In the West we may not be investing in capital, such as equipment and machines, anymore, but this isn't needed in order to be a high-tech knowledge economy. We don't have to build the machines and have the factories in our country to have a successful economy. We can design the machines and develop the technology, a prime example being the iPhone that is designed in the US but built in China. We can focus on the high value-add part of the process.

To achieve this we need to lead on technology through expenditure on research and development. This is spending to research new technologies, develop new products and discover new medicines. This leads to scientific and technological discoveries that are the true driver behind progress. So, are we doing this?

It is a mixed picture, but in general the West is not investing enough. Figure 2 shows expenditure by government, business and other entities on R&D. The euro area is spending only 2.1% of GDP on R&D. Then the UK has worryingly low R&D investment at 1.7%, down from 2.2% in the 1980s. The USA has relatively higher R&D investment at 2.8% of GDP, up modestly from 2.4% in the early 1980s. Higher again are the Scandinavian countries Sweden, Finland and Denmark that all spend more than 3% of GDP on R&D. It is perhaps no surprise that the US and Scandinavia have some of the strongest economies in the West, for it is new technology that drives economic growth in advanced economies.

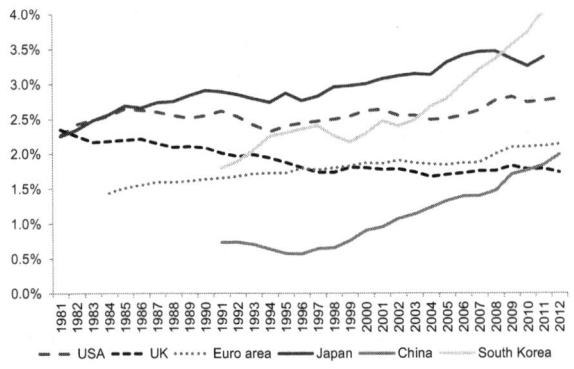

Figure 2. R&D expenditure as a percentage of GDP. Source: World Bank and OECD statistics.

More importantly, how does the West compare to the East? We are worryingly being outspent. China spent 2.0% of GDP on R&D in 2012, up from 0.7% in the early 1990s. In China's 2011/15 5-year plan it has targeted increasing this further to 2.5% by 2020. This is a high amount given that China has significantly lower GDP per capita than the West. Low-wage industries are typically not reliant on R&D, hence R&D spend normally rises in line with a country's income. We can see this in Figure 3, which shows R&D spend as a percent of GDP versus GDP/capita. This shows how China spends a high amount on R&D relative to its income level.

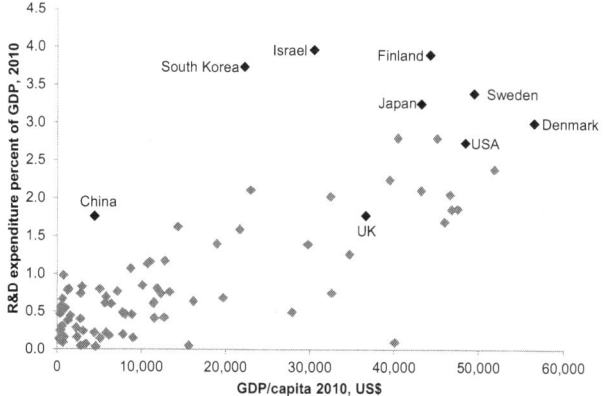

Figure 3. R&D expenditure as a percentage of GDP versus GDP per capita. Source: World Bank data.

The difference is more apparent when we compare ourselves to the richer Asian countries. South Korea increased R&D expenditure from 1.8% of GDP in 1991 to 4.0% in 2011. Japan also spends highly on R&D at 3.4% of GDP, up from 2.3% in the early 1980s.[3] Therefore Asia is spending significantly more than us on R&D and its R&D spend is increasing while in many Western countries it is at best rising modestly. Given this, it is hard to see how the West can maintain a lead in high-tech industries.

---

[3] R&D as a percentage of GDP from World Bank data and the OECD.

Our politicians often tell us that we will succeed in the global race not by having low wages, but by investing in technology to become a knowledge economy. The evidence provides little support for this rhetoric. Our companies are deciding to not invest and as such the West is starting to fall behind in key technologies.

We are already seeing the impact of this lack of investment in high-tech industries. Many people assume that the rise of the East, and specifically China, is solely due to low wages catching up with our own. This is an important part of China's rise, but it misses another critical development. Through its concerted investment China is beginning to lead in high-tech industries.

In telecoms I saw this first hand while working as a research analyst in an investment bank. I saw Chinese telecom equipment manufacturers' transition from being a low-cost alternative to being among the global technological leaders. This was revealed starkly when in 2013 I was at a presentation of a company rolling out a new mobile network in Europe. They were explaining why they had chosen certain pieces of equipment for each part of the network. For some parts they said technology had been less important so they had chosen the cheapest option, which in this case meant European manufacturers. Then for the parts where they wanted the best technology they chose one of the Chinese manufacturers. At the time I found this surprising, after doing the research for this book I find it totally expected.

A similar transition is taking place in green energy. We often hear about the very real pollution problem in China. What we don't hear about is that China is becoming a world leader in renewable energy. In 2013

China accounted for 21% of global investment in renewable energy.[4] In 2012 China produced 64% of global solar panels.[5] This is not simply manufacturing, the solar panels are being designed and made by Chinese companies. China has 7 of the top 10 solar panel manufacturers that are now leading on technology as well as production.

Another industry that China is beginning to take the lead on is, perhaps fittingly, the industry that started the first industrial revolution in the West, namely railways. 10 years ago China's railway companies were far behind the global leaders. Then between 2004 and the end of 2012 China built almost 10,000 km of high-speed railways, by which point China had almost 40% of the global high-speed train lines as measured by track length. Through this process they have become one of the world's leaders in high-speed trains. Over the next few years China will begin to export high-speed trains around the world.

These three examples of telecoms, solar power and railways show how the higher levels of investment are enabling China to take the lead in high-tech industries. If the West continues to underinvest it will continue to see high-tech industries move abroad. In the West it is companies that carry out the majority of investment, therefore it is of paramount importance to start them investing again.

---

[4] World Resources Institute (2013) "Renewable Energy in China: A Graphical Overview of 2013", China FAQs, The Network for Climate and Energy Information.
[5] International Renewable Energy Agency (2014) "Renewable Energy and Jobs, Annual Review 2014", May 2014.

If companies are not investing, where is the money going? Company management can decide to re-invest profits or return the money to shareholders. For the US there was a dramatic change in the early 1980s, this is shown in Figure 4. The proportion of profits paid out to shareholders increased from around 30% pre-1980 to an average of 100% after 1980. From the 1980s onwards companies shifted focus from investment to short-term profit and returning cash to shareholders. Companies shifted away from being the key conduits of investment in our economies, towards being a means of extracting profit. This shift typifies the problem of short-termism, why this happened in the 1980s will be explained in Chapters 3 and 4.

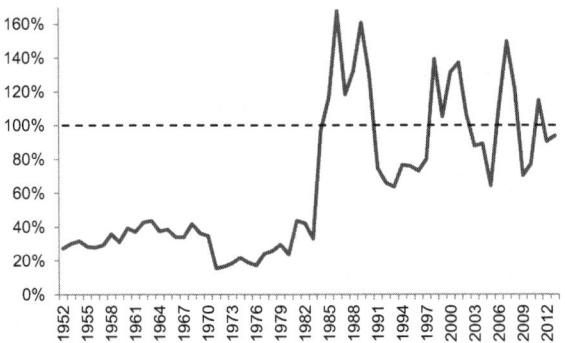

Figure 4. US cash returned to shareholders (via dividends and buybacks net of new equity issues) as a percentage of profit after tax. Source: Federal Reserve Z1 Table F.102

This leads to the next question, where do shareholders spend the money? If companies are returning cash to shareholders rather than investing, what are shareholders doing with the money? In aggregate the money flows through financial markets and is lent to governments that are running budget deficits. Essentially companies are not investing so are saving money, which is then being lent to the government.

The evidence for short-termism and a lack of investment is quite clear and as such there is growing recognition of it. This goes right across business, finance, politicians, regulators and academics. This is because, in contrast to many other complaints against business, short-termism makes almost everyone worse off. Other complaints against business are often framed as a battle between ordinary working people and business management, capital versus labour, greedy managers making excess profits at everyone else's expense. However, short-termism hurts everyone, without long-term investment there is no strong business to provide stable jobs, returns to investors are lower and our economy grows slower.

From finance and business there have been increasing calls from prominent figures that Western businesses need to act for the longer-term. The respected investor Warren Buffet was one of a long list of senior business and finance figures who signed a statement in 2009 calling for a longer-term approach by management and shareholders. Part of the statement said the following.[6]

> We believe a healthy society requires healthy and responsible companies that effectively pursue long-term goals. Yet in recent years, boards, managers, shareholders with varying agendas, and regulators, all, to one degree or another, have allowed short-term considerations to overwhelm the desirable long-term growth and

---

[6] Aspen Institute (2009) "Overcoming Short-termism: A Call for a More Responsible Approach to Investment and Business Management".

> sustainable profit objectives of the corporation. We believe that short-term objectives have eroded faith in corporations continuing to be the foundation of the American free enterprise system, which has been, in turn, the foundation of our economy. Restoring that faith critically requires restoring a long-term focus for boards, managers, and most particularly, shareholders—if not voluntarily, then by appropriate regulation.

In academia there is an increasing amount of literature that puts forward evidence of short-termism and proposes reforms. Politicians have also acknowledged the problem and have been commissioning countless reviews and trying to introduce some reforms. However, as we shall see later, the majority of these reforms have been too small. Reforms have too often simply tackled the specifics of the last scandal, rather than the underlying problem of short-termism.

This begs the question, why are we not able to deal with this? If removing the short-term focus benefits workers, investors and the economy, and if the problem is widely acknowledged; how come the situation is getting worse? The answer is that the interaction between management, shareholders and intermediaries has created a mutually reinforcing cycle of short-termism. For as much as any person or entity wants to break the cycle, it is very difficult to act alone, all elements of the system need to be reformed together. We cannot simply wish it away; we must reform the ownership and control of our companies. Only then will our companies start investing and by doing so will begin to benefit their investors, employees and the economy more broadly.

Conclusion

In the above chapter I have put the case that there is compelling evidence that short-termism is a major problem for the West. Our businesses are not investing enough and as such are losing out to longer-term focused Asian companies. Instead our businesses are focused on short-term profit and returning cash to shareholders. While this problem may be increasingly acknowledged, we are not yet doing enough about it. We focus all our attention on what politicians are doing and how much business leaders are earning, when the crucial question is, are our companies investing and in the right areas?

Chapter Two

Why Companies Exist

> *"The distinguishing facts, therefore, on which companies formed, are novelty of enterprise, uncertainty of the results and largeness of the means required for success."*
> —Robert Lowe ("Why Companies are Necessary", The Economist, 1856)

Why do we have companies? It is a simple question that we often ignore. Companies are now so ingrained in our society that we often forget they are a relatively recent development, only growing to dominate our economies in the late 19th century. Companies also had a controversial beginning, many prominent figures objected to their creation, even the father of economics, Adam Smith, was not a fan. To see what is broken with Western business we must first understand why we have companies. What vital function do they perform in our economy? And are they still doing this?

The answer to this question goes to the very core of human coordination and progress. Humanity is constantly presented with a range of activities to which it can engage. Some of these are quite simple and can be carried out by an individual, family or small group of people, for example farming a field, weaving cloth or working as a

2. Why Companies Exist

blacksmith. Other activities require large numbers of people working for long periods of time; to build a road or building, sail around the world in search of spices, send a man to the moon and research the cure for cancer.

Of this range of activities it is often the large, long-term and risky ones that make the biggest difference to progress. The problem is these projects are also the hardest to coordinate. Therefore a key determinant of success for a country has been its ability to coordinate large numbers of people to tackle these large, long-term and sometimes risky activities.

As humans we can coordinate quite well with each other on small tasks, if I need my lawn mowing I can pay someone to do this. Such free-market interactions organise a large amount of human activity. The problem is that large tasks require hundreds and thousands of people to coordinate with each other, which makes coordination much harder. The answer is that we pool resources and hence power into organisations that are then able to coordinate such activity.

We can see this with an analogy. Imagine there is a village that wants to build a bridge, but this will take 20 people 6 months to build. Therefore to build the bridge they need a pot of money large enough to pay 20 people for 6 months to complete the task. They could hold a town hall meeting to discuss plans and pass around a collecting jar, or maybe they could use crowd funding. However, we all know the meeting would likely end in chaos and the collecting jar would remain empty. Such simultaneous individual coordination is very difficult and unlikely to succeed.

There are a number of more successful alternatives. The government could build the bridge using money raised in taxes. A wealthy individual could agree to build it for charity or to charge per use and make a profit. Or a group of individuals could form a company, each investing a small amount and selecting someone to run the company and build the bridge. Lastly, all of these could be aided by a bank using people's savings to make a loan to help build the bridge.

Each of these alternatives involves creating a pool of resources with a singular decision point that is then able to coordinate activities to build the bridge. To coordinate on large, long-term and risky activities we need a mechanism to concentrate resources into an organisation or person. This can be the government, a wealthy individual, a bank or a company. These are all concentrations of power that have the ability to coordinate larger tasks.

We can see the role of concentrations of power through history, for until the last few hundred years the majority of the population worked in agriculture; this is best organised in small groups such as a family working a field. However, what really made a difference to a country was its ability to invest in infrastructure, fund trade missions and coordinate a large army. These could only be coordinated via governments, wealthy individuals, banks and companies.

Initially such tasks were coordinated by the government and associated ruling elite. The Egyptian's are famous for the pyramids, but the state also coordinated investment in complex irrigation systems. We likewise know Babylon for its hanging gardens, but again the state

2. Why Companies Exist

played a key role in irrigation investment, canals and helping organise large trade missions. The Phoenicians are famous for trading throughout the Mediterranean, this was enabled by close links between the merchants and the navy. Lastly, the Romans are famous for roads, sewers, grand buildings, extensive trade and a highly organised army.

We may not agree with the unfairness that results from power being concentrated into the hands of a few, but this has enabled coordination on activities that could never be accomplished by free-market interactions between individuals. However, relying solely on the state and wealthy individuals to coordinate large-scale activities had its limitations, power concentrated in the hands of a few people is eventually abused. There are countless examples throughout history of power being abused or wasted.

Centralising resources into one organisation enables large long-term and risky investments to be carried out, but these resources can also be wasted. We see this throughout history where large and powerful states have driven countries forwards through their ability to coordinate, but this power was eventually corrupted and abused. In the dying days of the Roman Empire inequality rose and the elite increasingly fought amongst themselves over the spoils of empire. A thousand years later the Chinese empire also turned inwards on itself, banning overseas trade for fear that this would destabilise the state's power. There are countless other examples.

This corruption of power constrained humanity for thousands of years. We could concentrate resources into the state to enable large long-term investment, but this would invariably lead to abuses of power and eventual downfall. The solution was to create rival organisations to the state, essentially mini-states within the state, concentrations of resources just big enough to carry out certain tasks, but not too big to carry out abuses of power. The answer was the company.

The first companies

From the early days of human civilisation there has been what we might recognise as companies. Around 2000 BC in Babylonia merchants would group together in an organisation called a *kāru*. There is even an example of merchants investing into a partnership that would engage in trade for 12 years and then distribute the profits.[1] In the Roman Empire merchants and craftsmen formed guilds ("collegia" or "corpora") that would elect a leader and coordinate activities.[2]

In 9th-century Italy, maritime traders would sometimes pool resources to fund a certain voyage, and hence spread the risk.[3] Then still in Italy in the 12th century organisations called *compagnia* started to form through which merchants would work together. As time went on these became more complex and attracted investors from outside the family.[4] However, these entities remained largely family affairs, relying on the bonds of kinship to hold the organisation together. They often rose and fell

---

[1] Karl Moore and David Lewis (2001) *Foundations of Corporate Empire*, 33.
[2] A.H.M Jones (1974) *The Roman Economy: Studies in Ancient Economic and Administrative History*.
[3] Fernand Braudel (1982) *Civilisation and Capitalism, 15th-18th Century. Vol II: The Wheels of Commerce*, New York: Harper&Row, 434.
[4] John Micklethwait and Adrian Wooldridge (2003) *The Company: A short history of a revolutionary idea*.

with the families that founded them and were still largely constrained by the wealth of the founding family.

It was only from the 16th century onwards that the modern company began to develop. Christopher Columbus had returned from "discovering" the Americas in 1493, Europe's age of overseas expansion was beginning. Merchants wanted to fund new trading routes, but the issue was that such trade missions were expensive and risky. The merchants needed a way to pool resources and spread the risk; the solution was the joint-stock company.

The first example was the Russia Company that formed in 1553 with exclusive rights to trade with Russia. Then The Virginia Company formed in 1584, raising money from 700 individuals to establish settlements in North America. This company funded the Pilgrims who travelled aboard the Mayflower. It also established the principle of self-government for the new settlements, but it did not deliver a return for investors. The most famous example from this period is the East India Company established in 1600 to trade with Asia. It delivered large returns for investors and wielded significant power. It expanded the British Empire into India, had its own standing army and its administrators were called civil servants before those in the state were.

These first companies in many ways resembled modern corporations, but they lacked one key part, which is limited liability. Up to this point commerce was organised by individuals working together in partnerships. These individuals had unlimited liability so would be liable for all debts the partnership incurred. In 1662 a crucial step was taken, the shareholders in a few companies were granted limited liability. This means if you invest £100 you can only lose £100. This would become the foundation stone of the modern corporation.

Limited liability greatly increased a company's ability to raise money from a large number of shareholders. Imagine in the recent financial crisis if there had been unlimited liability, shareholders would not just have lost the amount they invested, but would have also been liable for all the debt and mortgage write-downs. Such a system would understandably put many people off investing in companies. Hence limited liability did the opposite and enabled companies to have a large number of arms-length passive investors.

However, despite the success of the first joint-stock companies in overseas trade, not many were created. The majority of commerce continued to be conducted by families and small partnerships. There was a wave of company creations in the late 1600s, but these remained small. In 1695 six companies made up 75% of the total market value of listed companies in London, these were the Bank of England, the Million Bank, The New River Company (a water supplier in London) and 3 trading companies including the East India Company.[5] Most other activities in the economy did not need such large sums of money and so could be carried out by individuals and small partnerships.

Controversial beginnings

Then in the early 18th century there was a flurry of company incorporations and two of the most notorious

---

[5] William R. Scott (1912) *The Constitution and Finance of English, Scottish and Irish Joint-Stock Companies to 1720*, vol. 1.

financial bubbles in history; the South Sea Bubble in England and the Mississippi Madness in France. After expensive wars between 1689 and 1714 the French and English governments had built up considerable debts. To reduce the cost of this debt they both tried converting fixed-interest government debt into lower yielding shares in new companies. These companies had monopolies on trading with certain regions granted by the government. This led to a bubble in the value of these shares and an eventual crash in 1720. This collapsed the French economy, while England escaped more lightly.

The impact of the South Sea Bubble was to tarnish the idea of the company in many people's minds. England introduced the Bubble Act that required all joint-stock companies to be authorised by a royal charter. As such the majority of merchants and businessmen continued to prefer partnerships to joint-stock companies. It would be almost a hundred years before these concerns would be put aside and companies would resume their steady march to modern domination.

The main concern was that the combination of limited liability and hundreds of passive shareholders meant that no one was responsible for the actions of the company. People argued that creating a company as a separate legal entity removed all responsibility. This feeling is captured in a quote from Lord Chancellor Edward Thurlow (1731–1806) in England who said, "Corporations have neither bodies to be punished, nor souls to be condemned, they therefore do as they like".

With hundreds of shareholders there was little incentive for any one shareholder to monitor what management were doing. As a result management could abuse their power. Or management might lack the incentive to make the company succeed as an owner-entrepreneur would in a partnership. Some may find it surprising that Adam Smith, the father of economics, held this view and as such was not supportive of joint-stock companies. He wrote the following in *The Wealth of Nations*.[6]

> The directors of such [joint-stock] companies, however, being the managers rather of other people's money than of their own, it cannot well be expected, that they should watch over it with the same anxious vigilance with which the partners in a private copartnery frequently watch over their own... Negligence and profusion, therefore, must always prevail, more or less, in the management of the affairs of such a company.

As we shall see throughout this book, this is the same problem that we battle with today, and which through our desire to solve has led to the recent short-term focus. How are management monitored and held to account when you have hundreds of shareholders? Each shareholder is too small to influence management or to justify devoting such resources to doing so. Small shareholders are naturally passive, letting management run the company. If they disagree with management it is far easier to sell the shares than engage in the time consuming and costly exercise of trying to influence management. Economists call this the principal-agent problem, which I shall return to in the following chapter.

---

[6] Adam Smith (1776) *An Inquiry into the Nature and Causes of the Wealth of Nations*, Clarendon Press, Oxford, 741.

As a result of these concerns joint-stock companies had limited use through the 18th century, however with the industrial revolution in the 19th century this started to change. The industrial revolution required large upfront investments in canals, railways and factories. This created a demand for joint-stock companies to pool resources to make these large, long-term and often risky investments. The economy once again needed large concentrations of power and resources.

In many countries and especially in the UK there was a fierce debate on whether company incorporation should be made easier. The USA was one of the first to take such a step. In the USA corporate law is set by each state, the first state to allow automatic incorporation with limited liability was New York in 1811, though only for manufacturing businesses. Other states quickly followed, though company charters also had a set time period after which they would be reviewed by the state and only renewed if the state approved of the companies activities.

The UK was slower to make the move to automatic incorporation. Some companies even started to incorporate overseas to get around strict domestic laws. Eventually the Bubble Act introduced in 1720 after the South Sea Bubble was repealed in 1825, and with a subsequent series of acts automatic incorporation with limited liability status was introduced. As a result, between 1856 and 1862 25,000 companies were incorporated.[7] This wave of companies did lead to a fair dose of failure, 30% of the companies incorporated between 1856 and 1883 went bankrupt.

---

[7] John Micklethwait and Adrian Wooldridge (2003) *The Company: A short history of a revolutionary idea.*

The need for investment in railways and factories overcame people's concerns on the lack of responsibility caused by limited liability status. Companies enabled concentrations of resources to carry out large tasks such as overseas trade, building railways and utilities. They importantly did so not by relying on an increasingly powerful state or ruling class, but instead by creating rival concentrations of power. Each concentration of power being just big enough for the task it was created for.

Triumph for companies

Companies went on to fund successive rounds of investment in canals around 1800, mining 1820s, railways 1840s and electricity in the 1880s. However, manufacturing was still primarily carried out by small partnerships of individuals, especially in the UK. In general it was only railway companies and banks that were listed with hundreds of shareholders. It was only in the late 19th and early 20th century that large manufacturing companies started to form, in part driven by the increasing benefits of scale in new industries.

The USA led the move towards large manufacturing companies, with the UK lagging behind with an economy still dominated by small family-owned companies. In the US this process was partly driven by J.P. Morgan who used capital markets to consolidate industries, a famous example being when J.P. Morgan acquired Carnegie Steel in 1901, and then merged it with 200 other companies to form US Steel that controlled two thirds of American steel production.[8] This period saw the emergence of large companies called 'trusts' that dominated the US economy, such as John D. Rockefeller's Standard Oil that at its peak controlled 90% of US oil refining capacity. It was eventually broken up by Congress in 1911 into 33 smaller companies, two of which remain oil majors today, ExxonMobil and Chevron. During this period the US economy was dominated by large corporations.

The UK slowly followed down this same road, eventually creating large manufacturing companies. However, these tended to be in the old industries, rather than the new industries of metal, chemicals and machinery. The UK's slow move to large companies is shown by the fact that, in 1912, of the 100 largest industrial companies in the world by market capitalisation, 15 were headquartered in Britain compared to 54 in the US and 14 in Germany.[9] Germany appears low, but it had more private companies and gained the benefits of scale by companies working together in cartels.

In addition to the lack of large companies in new industries, UK companies paid out a significant proportion of earnings as dividends to shareholders, estimated at 80–90%, significantly higher than the US and Germany. We see the effect of this in the investment rates. Investment as a percentage of GDP was lower in the UK than the US. For 1870 to 1913 the UK invested on average 12% of GDP, compared to 23% in the USA.[10] It is perhaps

---

[8] John Micklethwait and Adrian Wooldridge (2003) *The Company: A short history of a revolutionary idea.*
[9] Brian R. Cheffins (2008) *Corporate Ownership and Control*, Oxford University Press, 178.
[10] Gross fixed capital formation as a percentage of GDP calculated from data collated and made available by Thomas Piketty.

of little surprise that the UK began its relative economic decline during this period. This was an early sign that companies could move away from the reason for their existence, which is to invest.

The gates had been opened and companies steadily grew to dominate every aspect of our economy, enabling investment and coordination on a much larger scale than could ever have been possible with small partnerships.

Conclusion

In this chapter I argued that an important part of progress comes from the ability to coordinate large, long-term and often risky projects. We can only achieve this by concentrating resources, power and money into organisations with a singular decision point. For most of human history this has been the state and ruling elite. However, the problem with states is that power is eventually abused.

The formation of companies enabled rival organisations to form within a country. It created multiple concentrations of power in society, each created to carry out a specific task. This enabled the benefits of large-scale coordination with a much lower risk that power was abused. As a result companies enabled investment in overseas trade in the 1600s and then railways in the mid-19th century, before expanding to the whole economy in the late 19th century.

Companies provide a means to concentrate resources to pursue those opportunities that make the biggest difference to our society and economy, therefore the current short-term focus risks subverting the very purpose that lay behind the company's creation, which was to invest.

Chapter Three

Ownership and Control

"On the face of it, shareholder value is the dumbest idea in the world."
— Jack Welch, CEO General Electric 1981–2001

By the early 20th century Western economies were increasingly dominated by large listed companies, in many ways resembling our current economy. However, there was a key difference; most companies were still controlled by a few large shareholders, often the founding families. They may have floated the company, bringing in outside investors, but they retained a controlling stake. The exception being railway companies and banks which already had quite diffuse ownership. Over the following hundred years the ownership and control of companies steadily evolved towards our modern structure with its unfortunate short-term focus, this story is the focus of this chapter.

In the early 20th century as the control of companies rested with the large controlling shareholders, there were limited rights for the small minority shareholders. The understanding was that the controlling shareholders ran the company and outsiders could buy shares if they wanted, but should not expect any influence. The protection for such minority shareholders was often simply reputation. Disclosure was also very low, investors often only had the dividend on which to base a valuation. Concentrations of resources may have expanded beyond what was possible with families and partnerships, but control still rested with a few individuals.

After the First World War (WWI) this started to change as the controlling families began to sell out and more people wanted to buy shares. As a result of this the ownership and control of companies in the UK and US began to separate. Companies increasingly had no controlling shareholder, but instead a large number of small shareholders.

In the UK a study of companies in 1920 found that the average largest shareholder had a 21% stake.[1] A similar study of companies in 1936 found that this had fallen to 10.3%.[2] The US saw an even greater separation of ownership and control in this period. The seminal study by Berle and Means in 1932 looked at 200 non-financial companies and found that 45% had diffuse ownership and hence with no one shareholder in control.[3]

The separation of ownership and control continued after WWII, with the UK catching up with the US. A study replicating Berle and Mean's work in 1963 found

---

[1] Julian Franks, Colin Mayer and Stefano Rossi (2006) "Ownership: Evolution and Regulation", ECGI Fin. Working Paper No.09/2003, 19, Table 2.

[2] P. Sargant Florence (1953) *The Logic of British and American Industry: A Realistic Analysis of Economic Structure and Government*, 187-9. It should be noted that this study ignored banks and railways that already had quite diffuse ownership.

[3] Berle and Means (1932) *The Modern Corporation and Private Property*.

that the proportion of companies with no controlling shareholder in the US had increased to 85% (from 45% in 1932).[4] This trend also continued in the UK, such that by 1970 only 30 of the top 100 industrial companies were under family control.[5] While some studies have disputed the extent to which ownership and control were separated in the US and UK, the majority of opinion and evidence find that it was.[6]

Why ownership and control separated in UK and US companies has been a key focus for academic debate for some time. One reason was the falling inequality provided the middle class with sufficient wealth to buy shares. It is estimated that the number of individuals owning shares in the UK doubled between the start of the 20th century and 1939.[7] The fall in inequality is shown in Figure 5, which shows the share of national income that went to the top 10% of earners. Other reasons vary from the tax structure favouring listed companies, companies increasing in size, greater legal protections for small shareholders and lower political support for trade unions.

The reasons why are not important for the discussion here. The important point is that companies were no longer controlled by a few large shareholders. Instead hundreds of shareholders elected a board of directors who ran the company. This led to very different incentives and frameworks for how decisions were made.

---

[4] Larner, R.J., "Ownership and Control in the 200 Largest Non-financial Corporations, 1929 and 1963", *American Economic Review*, 56, 777–87.
[5] Derek F.Channon (1973) *Strategy and Structure of British Enterprise*, 22, 75.
[6] Brian Cheffins and Steven Bank (2009) "Is Berle and Means Really a Myth?", *Business History Review*, 83 (3), Autumn, 443–74.
[7] Brian Cheffins (2010) *Corporate Ownership and Control*, Oxford University Press, 270.

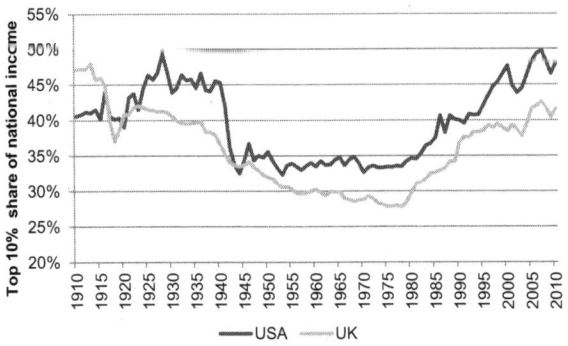

Figure 5. Top 10% share of national income. Source: Thomas Piketty, "Capital in the 21st Century" and corresponding WTID database.

Managerial capitalism

The problem with the separation of ownership and control is that the legal frameworks had been developed for companies that had a small number of controlling shareholders and gave limited rights to the smaller minority shareholders. But now that there were no controlling shareholders there was little means for any shareholders to exercise influence. Boards of directors became full of senior management and those connected to senior management. It was difficult for a shareholder who only owned a few percent to exercise any influence at all.

This is called the principal-agent problem by economists and is the same as the concern expressed by Adam Smith about companies 150 years earlier. How can shareholders ensure that management will act in their interests? How can management be encouraged to act as if they were the owners of the business? Who is held responsible for a company? These questions have plagued companies from their very inception.

3. Ownership and Control

The shareholders (the principal) want to appoint a manager (the agent) to run the company for them, as they cannot do it themselves. The problem is that the shareholders cannot monitor everything the manager is doing and so cannot know for sure if management are acting in their interests, this is technically known as asymmetric information. Then in addition management may have different incentives to the shareholders. Management may prefer a comfortable life enjoying the corporate perks, rather than working hard to increase the value of the business.

The problem is that for a shareholder there is a cost in terms of time and resources to monitor and influence management. For a large shareholder it generally makes sense to do so, they have more money on the line and a greater ability to influence management. However, with a large number of small shareholders the cost of trying to influence management is too high versus the size of stake they hold. They would prefer to avoid such a costly exercise and for another shareholder to monitor management. As a result all the shareholders do nothing and management can run the company as they wish.

The downside of this is captured by Berle and Means in their 1932 seminal book: "The property owner who invests in a modern corporation so far surrenders his wealth to those in control of the corporation that he has exchanged the position of independent owner for one in which he may become merely recipient of the wages of capital… [such owners] have surrendered the right that the corporation should be operated in their sole interest…"[8]

---

[8] A. Berle and G. Means (1932) *The Modern Corporation and Private Property*.

The separation of ownership and control in the US and UK led to what is termed "managerial capitalism". Management controlled the company and decided who was on the board of directors. Shareholders all held stakes too small to have any influence and therefore took a very passive role. This is the essence of the principal-agent problem. Shareholders had very little means to ensure that management were acting in their interest. The UK and US broadly functioned like this for the 50s, 60s and 70s.

As a result profit was not the primary focus. While the shareholder was still legally paramount, this was not the perception or practice. The purpose of companies was seen as serving all stakeholders such as employees and customers as well as shareholders. This is captured by an article in *The Economist* in 1953 that said, "[shareholders] rank well after the employees, the progress of 'the company', and the wellbeing of the customer in the thoughts of the directors whom—in legal form—they appoint".[9] This was further supported by the cultural and political discourse at the time being one of solidarity after WWII.

This situation provided little incentive for management to perform. Management pay was broadly fixed and simply based on the size of the company. Commentary at the time paints the picture well for the UK saying there was "a certain claret-grouse-and-port induced somnolence in British boardrooms",[10] with "the unconscious ambition of most directors to retire and

---

[9] "The Shareholder Today", *The Economist*, 19th December 1953, 903–4.
[10] Charles Raw (1977) *Slater Walker: An Investigation of a Financial Phenomenon*, 170, quoting fortune, June 1973.

become country squire".[11] This was arguably due to a lack of incentives for management due to little incentive pay and extremely high levels of taxation. As highlighted in an article in *The Times* in 1970, "Managers have little incentive for risk taking, or even for a busier life at all when the net rewards are so small".[12]

This problem was particularly acute in the UK, and it arguably continued the UK's relative economic decline that had started in 1870. The cause was also the same as before; that British businesses were run poorly. Around the year 1900 this had been levelled at family owners running businesses simply to maintain a certain lifestyle, paying out profits in dividends rather than reinvesting. After WWII this criticism was directed at management who all sat on each other's boards and wanted a certain standard of life, rather than to drive their businesses to succeed.

While the problem was worse in the UK, it was felt across most Western economies. Control of companies had transitioned from founding families to professional managers who had little incentive to increase the share price. Instead management had an incentive to build a corporate empire. The concerns voiced by Adam Smith in 1776 were now widely evident.

Rise of institutional investors

During the 60s and 70s there was an equally dramatic development occurring in how people saved that had the potential to solve the problems caused by the separation

---

[11] George Norman (1973) "The English Sickness", *Bankers' Magazine*, November, 192, 195.
[12] "The Executive and British Tax", *The Times*, 25th August 1970.

of ownership and control. Share ownership steadily transitioned from individuals to institutional investors such as pension funds, insurance companies and mutual funds. Increasingly individuals did not own shares directly, but instead through their savings in a pension fund or other investment vehicle.

In the 1930s 80% of UK shares were owned by individuals, including those with large controlling stakes. By 1962 this had fallen to 54% and by 2012 to 11%, as shown in Figure 6. This gap has been filled by domestic institutional investors and more recently by foreign institutions. Foreign institutions now own over 50% of UK shares, partly because US asset managers acquired a number of UK asset managers, and hence these investments are often still managed from offices in London.

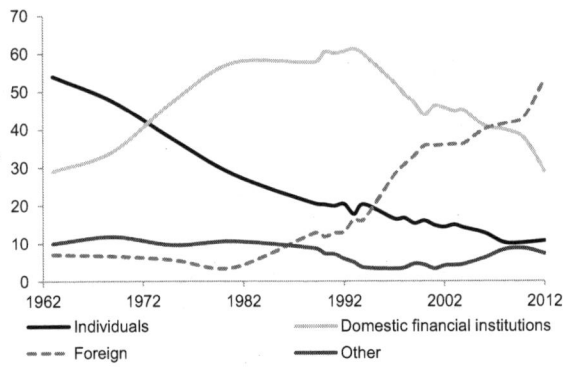

Figure 6. Beneficial ownership of UK shares. Source: ONS Share Ownership 2012, DEYF-DEYP.

In the UK this rapid transfer from individual shareholders to institutions was primarily driven by the tax system that penalised individuals but benefited institutions. For example, contributions to pension funds are made before income tax and the pension fund itself does not pay income tax or capital gains tax. This was in stark contrast to high marginal tax rates on individuals in the 60s and 70s. Estimates for high income earners in the UK put the tax rate on dividends near 70% in the 1970s.[13] As a result the proportion of personal wealth directly held in equities dropped from 22% in 1957 to 9% in 1976.[14] This led to a significant increase in pension funds. The percentage of workers with a pension scheme in the UK rose from 13% in 1936 to around 50% in the 1960s and 1970s.[15]

A similar development happened in the USA, see Figure 7. The proportion of US shares owned by US individuals fell from 93% in 1945 to 25% in 2007. The proportion owned by US institutional investors rose from 3% to 57%, driven by pension funds and mutual funds. There was a more modest rise in foreign investors from 2% to 13%. Tax changes were again a significant contributing factor in the growth of pension funds and mutual funds. Only when an individual receives a dividend from a mutual fund or sells is tax paid.

The rise in institutional investors had the potential to solve the issues caused by the separation of ownership and control. Thousands of small individual shareholders found it very difficult to influence management, but if everyone invested through large funds then these would have the size and resources to act as controlling shareholders. Similar to the controlling families in the early 20th

---

[13] Cheffins, *supra*, 342.
[14] Cheffins, *supra*, 343.
[15] Leslie Hannah (1986) *Inventing Retirement: The Development of Occupational Pensions in Britain*, 66–7.

century, they could ensure that management ran the company for the shareholders rather than themselves.

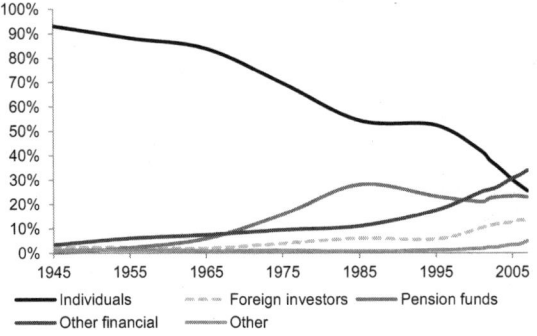

Figure 7. US listed companies share ownership. Source: Gregory Jackson, "Understanding Corporate Governance in the United States"—US Federal Reserve, Flow of Funds Accounts.

Some even called this the beginning of "pension fund socialism". Through pension funds the workers were starting to own the capital of the country. This was in effect decentralised socialism with the workers finally owning the means of production. This was supported by lower wealth inequality that had been falling since 1910. The prominent management consultant and author Peter Drucker, who is described by some as the founder of modern management theory, encapsulated this idea in his 1976 book, *The Unseen Revolution*.[16] The book says that, as of 1976, American workers owned one third of US companies, and that this could rise to two thirds by the year 2000. In the end only a few years later quite the

---

[16] Peter Drucker (1976) *The Unseen Revolution*.

opposite happened. The 1980s turned out to be what is now called the "deal decade".

The deal decade

The 1980s saw a reversal of many trends in Western economies. Wealth and income inequality started to rise again. As a result pension fund share ownership in the US peaked, outpaced by the wealthy investing in mutual funds. The large industrial conglomerates were broken up. Trade union membership collapsed. CEO pay increased dramatically, while real wages stagnated. The growth of institutional investors did shift the focus of management onto shareholder value, but the outcome could hardly be described as pension fund socialism.

Investors had happily taken a passive stance during the long economic boom in the 50s and 60s. They had no need to influence management if profits and dividends were growing. But with the 1970s came an economic crisis and rising competition from the likes of Japan. Western companies looked increasingly weak and in need of reform. Investors were becoming fed up with the basis of "managerial capitalism" where managers did not exclusively focus on shareholder value. Complaints about the age-old principal-agent problem resurfaced once again.

A prime example of this was the conglomerates that had formed in the 50s and 60s. These were large companies engaged in a range of unrelated activities. In the 50s and 60s management pay had been broadly based on the size of the company, hence managers acquired unrelated businesses in a process of empire building. One example in the US was Ling-Temco-Vought that had businesses ranging from aeroplanes to sports goods, car rentals and pharmaceuticals. Or Gulf+Western that had businesses ranging from clothing to manufacturing, music and sugar.

The share price of these conglomerates began to reflect the lack of focus on shareholder value. The value of their shares traded at less than the value of all their separate parts. Therefore an opportunity arose for buy-out funds to acquire the conglomerates and sell them off piece by piece at a higher price. This then went beyond conglomerates to any company where management were not acting in shareholders' interests. The buy-out funds would acquire the company, change the management team, shift the focus onto shareholder value and then sell at a profit.

As a result there was a boom in hostile take-overs, as shown in Figure 8 and as was encapsulated in the iconic film *Wall Street*. Prior to the 1980s, take-overs were "not the done thing" in the cosy world of 50s and 60s boardrooms. Perhaps surprisingly it was only in 1974 that an investment bank advised on a hostile take-over for the first time, when they are now synonymous with such activity. Take-overs were further enabled by new forms of financing such as junk bonds.

The exact cause of the 'deal decade' is hotly debated, but broadly there was a growing desire from investors to influence management, to make them focus on shareholder value. Then there was an increasing capability to influence management due to the growth in buy-out funds and junk bonds. As a result, management either focused on shareholder value, or their company would be taken over and they would be out of a job.

Figure 8. Number of hostile takeover bids in the USA and UK. Source: Gregory Jackson, "Understanding Corporate Governance in the US", Hans-Böckler-Foundation (2010).

The 1980s has its proponents and detractors. There were examples of corporate excess and greed, companies taken over and broken up just to make a short-term profit. But on the other hand it also reorganised the economy, moving away from large conglomerates operating in many industries, towards companies with much greater scale in one specific industry. For all that was wrong with the 1980s, it arguably realigned Western company structures to create the global champions that drove economic success in the 1990s.

However, whether you agree with the changes in the 1980s or not, what is important here is that it fundamentally shifted the focus of Western business onto shareholder value.

Share based compensation

In response to the take-over boom in the 1980s, management sought to re-align themselves with shareholders, moving away from "managerial capitalism" and focusing on shareholder value. A significant part of this was the increase in executive pay linked to the share price. Management increasingly aligned their incentives with shareholders through share option schemes. For example, in the US the value of stock options as a proportion of CEO pay increased from 10% in 1980 to 48% in 1994.[17] Some estimate that the sensitivity of CEO pay to performance increased by tenfold from 1980 to 1998.[18]

Shareholders also did not want management to resist take-overs, as owning shares in a company that was taken over delivered high returns for shareholders. Therefore "golden parachute" clauses were introduced in many senior management contracts, to guarantee them a large pay-out in the event of a take-over. Management therefore became just as keen as shareholders to be bought out at a high price. In the US such "golden parachute" clauses were in place at 41% of the largest 1,000 firms in 1988, and continued to spread to 57% in 1996 and 70% in 2000.[19]

This realignment through management pay was not the result of a battle between company management and shareholders, for as a result of these changes management pay increased significantly. Management did not

---

[17] Hall, B. and Liebman, J. (1998) "Are CEOs Really Paid like Bureaucrats?", *Quarterly Journal of Economics*, 112, 653–91.

[18] Bengt Holmstrom and Steven N. Kaplan (2003) "The State of U.S. Corporate Governance: What's Right and What's Wrong?", 15, *J. Applied Corporate Finance*, 8 (Spring 2003).

[19] Jensen, M.C. and Murphy, K.J. (2004) "Remuneration: Where we've been, how we got to here, what are the problems, and how to fix them", ECGI – Finance Working Paper, 44/July 2004.

need much of a prod from the threat of take-overs to encourage them to introduce share price based pay schemes. In the US, executive pay had been around 40 times the average worker's salary between 1950 and 1980. This increased to 140 times in 1991 and 500 times in 2003.[20] The UK saw a similar development, though on a lower scale, with executive pay to average worker pay increasing from 45 to 120 times from 1998 to 2010.[21]

Alongside this change in pay structures was a change in the composition of the board of directors. During the days of managerial capitalism boards had been full of people connected to senior management. Management would appoint each other to their respective boards, creating a rather cosy club. As shareholders demanded more accountability from management the proportion of board members with no connection to management increased. These are called independent directors and Figure 9 shows how they increased in US companies. Along with share based compensation this shifted the focus of companies firmly onto increasing shareholder value.

---

[20] Janice Ravel (2003) "Mo' Money, Fewer Problems: Is it a Good Idea to Get Rid of the $1 Million CEO Pay Ceiling?", *Fortune*, 31st March.
[21] Steven Bloomfield (2013) *Theory and Practice of Corporate Governance and Integrated Approach.*

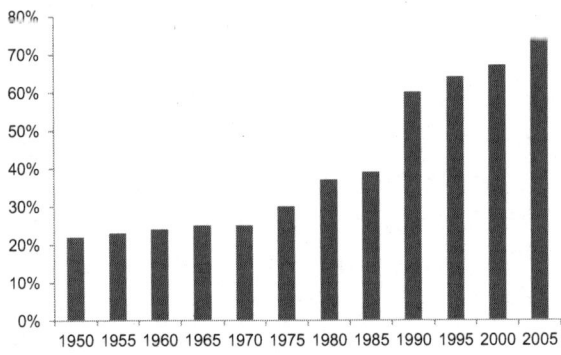

Figure 9. Proportion of US board of directors who were independent. Source: Gordon (2007)[22]

Conclusion

In this chapter we've seen how companies transitioned from being owned and controlled by a few families to having diffuse individual share ownership in the 1920s and 30s. This led to "managerial capitalism" in the 1950s, 60s and 70s, where shareholders had little influence and hence management ran companies with all stakeholders in mind and built conglomerate empires. This typifies the principal-agent problem where shareholders could not ensure that management ran the company to increase shareholder value.

During this period there was also a large transition in share ownership from individuals to institutional investors, such as pension funds. In the 1980s there was a wave of take-overs and the focus of management shifted firmly onto shareholder value. To further align incentives management pay was increasingly linked to the share

---

[22] Gordon, J.N. (2007) The Rise of Independent Directors in the United States, 1950–2005: Of shareholder value and stock market prices, *Stanford Law Review*, 59, 1465–568.

price. This may have appeared to be the solution to the age-old principal-agent problem, but as we shall see in the next chapter this was the foundation of the current short-term focus.

Chapter Four
Rise of Short-Termism

> *"The dominance of short-term perspectives has led to routine decisions in the markets that sacrifice the long-term build-up of genuine value in pursuit of artificial, short-term gains."*
> — Al Gore

Linking management compensation to the share price appears to be an ideal solution to the age-old principal-agent problem. It creates an incentive for management to act in the interests of shareholders and provides them with an incentive to succeed. It has successfully focused management on shareholder value but, as we shall see in this chapter, it has done so in a perverse way, skewing incentives to the short-term. We shall see how this is due to a vicious cycle of mutually reinforcing short-term incentives for all those involved. This is causing our companies to underinvest, which in turn is accelerating the relative economic decline of the West.

How shareholders influence management

The problem starts with the way that shareholders gained influence over management. There were no big legal changes in the 1980s providing shareholders with more power to influence management. As we saw in the last chapter, the shareholder was still legally paramount during the days of "managerial capitalism" in the 50s and 60s. Instead shareholders gained power by influencing the share price, which in turn impacts management's share-based compensation and the risk of being taken over.

There are two broad ways that shareholders can influence management—direct legal channels, or indirectly via the share price. Using direct legal channels involves voting at the annual general meeting (AGM). This is an annual meeting for the shareholders to vote on certain areas such as approving the financial results, dividend and electing the board of directors. At the AGM the board of directors also present to the shareholders how the company has performed over the last year and answer any questions.

Therefore to influence management a shareholder could try to elect someone to the board of directors at the AGM, or they could pass a motion requesting that management take a certain action. Or recently votes have been introduced on management pay at the AGM, called say-on-pay in the US, introduced in the Dodd-Frank Act in 2010.

There are some instances of shareholders voting against management at the AGM, trying to remove directors, change strategic decisions or increase the dividend. These events naturally capture attention, they are however quite rare. The AGM for most companies is a formality. Most investors either vote with management or sell their shares, which is known as the 'Wall Street Rule'. There has been a growth in activist funds, who buy shares and then seek to influence management. However, they often rely on open letters to management requesting a certain action, they less frequently mount a full challenge at the AGM.

The reason shareholders rarely use a direct legal means to influence management is because it is very difficult and time consuming. As a small shareholder it rarely makes sense to devote significant time to influencing management. The effort will generally be unsuccessful. Therefore if shareholders disagree with what management are doing they generally sell.

The decision of shareholders to buy and sell is the second means to influence management. If a shareholder sells their shares then this will push the share price down. This will reduce management's pay which is linked to the share price performance. This will also make the company more vulnerable to a take-over. Therefore management listen carefully to what shareholders are saying because they want a high share price, not in general because of potential votes at the AGM.

In addition to management pay, the share price has become the main way that we assess the performance of companies. Companies with high valuations are deemed to be successful and management doing a good job. Management don't just care about monetary reward, they want the respect of their peers, and since the 1980s this has increasingly been determined by the share price.

Therefore the 1980s gave significant influence to shareholders and financial markets over company decisions, but it did this via the indirect means of share prices and management pay, rather than the legal route of voting at the AGM.

4. Rise of Short-Termism

Short-term management compensation

Influence via the share price by itself is not a problem. The issue is what determines the share price and over what time period management are paid. Most management teams have what is called a long-term incentive plan, which rewards them for the rolling 3-year share price performance. This is far shorter than the investment cycle of the typical business and far shorter than the time horizon of an entrepreneur owner who plans to run the company their whole life and maybe even pass it onto their children.

The average investment cycle for most companies is much longer than 3 years. An oil company may take 10 years to develop a new oil field, which will then produce oil for 50 years. Car companies take at least 2 years to develop a new car, then years to recoup this investment. Management make a large number of decisions for which success will only be known after much longer than 3 years.

Further to this, a 3-year scheme becomes a 1- and 2-year scheme as it nears completion, therefore the short-term focus is even greater. CEOs are on average in their job for 6 years and therefore will only complete three incentive schemes, schemes only pay out if still employed through the 3 years. Of these schemes one may have started with a particularly favourable share price, perhaps there was a market wobble when the start of the scheme was priced. Therefore the CEO's incentives are often weighted to one of these schemes, worsening the short-term focus.

Therefore management are being paid long before the eventual outcome of the decisions they make. They are being paid based on the expectation of the decisions they make. Imagine if footballers were paid at half time based on the expectation of whether they would win the game or not. We would expect some pretty confident speeches assuring victory, followed by some lacklustre second half performances. We will see how it is payment based on expectations, rather than outcomes, which causes such problems when combined with other short-term biases.

The problem of short-term pay schemes is then accentuated by the falling tenure of CEOs. Management actions cannot be as long-sighted if they are in their jobs for shorter and shorter periods of time. Management are completing fewer full cycles of their already short 3-year incentive schemes. For the world's largest 2,500 companies CEO tenure has fallen from just less than 10 years in 1995 to 6 years in 2009.[1,2]

The importance of having the same CEO for a long time is shown by English football clubs. English football clubs have a very high turnover of managers, the average tenure was 1½ years in 2010, half what it was in 1993. During this period (1993–2010), of the 92 clubs in the English football leagues only two had the same manager for significantly longer than this, Sir Alex Ferguson at Manchester United and Arsene Wenger at Arsenal. These two clubs won the Premier League in 75% of the years in

---

[1] Favaro, K., Karlsson, P. and Neilson, G.L. (2010) "CEO Succession 2000–2009: A Decade of Convergence and Compression", *Strategy+Business* 59, Booz & Company.

[2] Karlsson, P., Neilson, G.L. and Webster, J.C. (2007) "CEO Succession 2007: The Performance Paradox", *Strategy+Business* 51, Booz & Company.

this period.[3] Long-term tenure and long-term action has its benefits.

Share prices reflect the short-term

The short-term time period of management compensation is not necessarily a problem. On its own this might not lead to short-termism. The problem comes from the combination of short-term management pay with a number of other biases.

A share price reflects expectations on the future success and profitability of a company. A share price is technically the net present value of all future dividends and hence profit for a company. A company may have a low profit that is expected to increase with a new product they are developing, or high dividend that is expected to fall as its technology is becoming obsolete. Therefore in theory share prices reflect the future and hence the long-term implications of all management decisions.

Let us assume the perfect case that share prices reflect the long-term implications of all management decisions. If a manager engaged in over-zealous cost cutting then the share price would fall due to the damage done to the business, rather than rise due to higher short-term profits. Or if a company was underpaying staff, the share price would fall to reflect a lack of talent and motivation that would slowly develop. Or, with a sufficiently long-term horizon, companies not preparing for the impact of climate change might have a lower share price. This could encourage oil companies to develop renewable energy and car companies to develop electric cars. In such a

---

[3] Andrew Haldane (2010) "Patience and Finance", paper for *Oxford China Business Forum*, 21.

scenario it would not matter if company management had very short-term incentives because the share prices would reflect long-term outcomes.

Many people view share trading as a large casino, but the above scenario shows the important role share trading can play in company decisions. Through the process of share trading, management actions are assessed by hundreds of analysts and fund managers. Then, through the decisions to buy and sell shares, this provides feedback to management. This process of analysis and share trading creates an open and immediate cross-check on management that in theory should reflect all long-term impacts. The analysis conducted by analysts and fund managers should form an important and vital role in how companies are run and how capital is allocated in our economy.

There is a catch though in that share prices do not reflect the long-term impact of all management decisions; there is instead a short-term bias. This should be no surprise, the future is uncertain and investors do not have a crystal ball. Therefore investors rely on the company's reported profit as the main indication of the value of a company. Shareholders and analysts try to go further than this, to forecast what profits will be in the future. But the valuation of shares is still significantly driven by short-term financial results. The further into the future we look the more the outcomes are uncertain and therefore valuations focus on what is more certain, which is the short-term.

Management know more than shareholders

The short-term focus of share prices is again not necessarily a problem on its own. The future will always be uncertain. No one knows exactly what will happen tomorrow, whether they are analysts, shareholders or management. The fact our decisions are biased towards the here and now is a fact of human life. The problem is that short-termism is compounded because management know far more about their business than any outsiders. Economists call this asymmetric information.

Management know if a technology is nearing the end, if cost-cutting has gone too far or if something is a significant risk to the business. In contrast investors and analysts only have public information to assess a company and a short amount of time to do so. As a consequence there is a significant information gap between investors and management. Investors find it hard to know if profits are rising for the right reasons.

This information gap creates an incentive for management to make decisions that will push the share price up even if they know this will damage the long-term success of the business. This might be excessive cost-cutting, reducing long-term investment or taking on a dangerously high amount of debt. If a CEO's share scheme will pay out based on the share price in 2 years and they expect to leave after this point, then they have a strong incentive to push the share price up into this point.

The problem is that management are paid based on the expected outcome of the decisions they take. It is relatively easy for management to increase profits by excessive cost-cutting and underinvestment. It is then difficult for outsiders to determine if rising profit is a sign of success or bad management decisions. There was even a survey in 2005 of US business leaders in which 78% said they would be willing to reduce discretionary spending on research and development, advertising and hiring in order to meet earnings benchmarks.[4]

Therefore the combination of these three factors feed on each other to create short-termism; short-term share-based management compensation, share prices that are based on short-term outcomes and an information gap between management and shareholders. This creates an incentive for management to make decisions that push the share price up in the short-term, in order to receive higher compensation, even if this is to the detriment of the business longer-term.

Investor short-term focus

Short-termism is further compounded by an increasingly short-term focus for investors, which increases the degree to which share prices reflect short-term outcomes. For example, for UK listed companies the average period of time a shareholder holds their shares has fallen from 5 years in the 1960s to 2 years in the 1980s and then 7.5 months in 2007.[5] This decline is partly accentuated by a small proportion of high frequency traders, but the overall decline in investment horizons is hard to refute. It is not surprising that we have a short-term focus if shareholders on average are holding shares for only 12 months or less.

---

[4] Graham, J., Harvey, C. and Rajgopal, S. (2005) "The Economic Implications of Corporate Financial Reporting", *Journal of Accounting and Economics*, 40: 1–3, 3–73.

[5] London Stock Exchange data in Andrew Haldane (2010) "Patience and Finance", paper for *Oxford China Business Forum*, 21.

The shortening of investor horizons has been caused by a number of factors, but most importantly by another principal-agent relationship, this time between fund managers and the investors in their funds. As we saw in the previous chapter the majority of shares are now owned by institutional investors such as pension funds and mutual funds. The individuals investing in these funds often have long-term horizons. For example a 35-year-old saving for their pension has 30 years before they will start to draw down on their savings when they retire. The problem is by investing through a fund the investment horizon is reduced to a few months.

This is shown most clearly for a pension fund. The fund is administered by a board of trustees elected by all the pension fund members. The trustees then allocate the money to different investment funds to manage the money. The trustees want to ensure the fund managers are doing a good job and are suitably incentivised, so they'll look for funds where the fund manager is paid based on performance. The trustees will also monitor the performance and if it is weak they may transfer money out into another fund. For example in the UK 66% of pension funds review the performance of fund managers every quarter or less.[6] Therefore through the desire to incentivise and hold fund managers to account, the investment outlook is shortened from 30 years for the average pension fund saver, to only a few months.

I recently heard another prime example of this. One of the world's largest asset managers recently had a new

---

[6] Aviva (2011) "The Kay Review of UK Equity Markets and Long-Term Decision Making Aviva Investor response to the Call for Evidence", Nov 2011.

head appointed. One of the first changes they made was to introduce monthly performance assessment for all fund managers. All fund managers now have to send a report once a month detailing the last month's performance and why it was good or bad. The desire to pay for performance and to closely monitor those who manage our savings is quite understandable. However, it creates a dangerously short-term focus in those who are deciding how our savings are invested, which in turn leads to short-term decisions in our companies and economy.

For fund managers these short-term incentives and performance assessment create an incentive to invest in shares that are expected to deliver a quick profit. Imagine there are two companies; one has developed a new technology that at some point over the next 10 years may replace petrol cars. The other company is likely to increase its dividend at its results announcement next month. The underlying pension saver with a 30-year horizon may prefer to invest in the technology company, but the fund manager with monthly performance assessments to worry about will invariably pick the company with the expected dividend increase.

Therefore the short-term performance assessment of fund managers puts a focus on short-term share price catalysts. This in turn means that share prices reflect short-term expectations, rather than long-term potential impacts. Climate change may have a large impact long-term, but if there are no short-term catalysts it will not drive short-term share prices and hence will be ignored by most fund managers.

The short-term focus of fund managers increases the degree to which share prices reflect short-term expectations which, together with short-term share-based management compensation, encourages short-term decisions by management. We should not blame the fund managers or management; it is just the result of structures put in place to assess performance and solve the principal-agent problem. An understandable desire for accountability leads to targets and performance assessment that leads to short-term decisions.

Short-term focused research

Another reason for the short-term focus of share prices comes from how research is carried out in the market. The decisions to buy and sell shares are based on detailed research into the future prospects of companies. The quality of this research determines the degree to which share prices reflect the long-term impact of management's decisions. It is relatively easy to see what the impact will be tomorrow, but it takes an onerous amount of analysis to predict what might happen further into the future. Only if investment decisions are based on such high quality analysis will share prices reflect long-term prospects and hence improve management decisions.

Perhaps surprisingly the majority of research and analysis is not carried out by the fund managers, but is instead provided by intermediaries, predominantly investment banks, called sell-side research. Therefore the entities that run financial markets also write the research about them. Unsurprisingly this has led to a swathe of problems. Imagine if the politicians controlled the press how objective that would be. This has led to a number of scandals and most problematically I argue creates a short-term bias.

This short-term bias arises from the way that investment banks are paid for research. Investment banks are primarily paid for research when investment funds buy and sell shares through the bank. Hence there is an incentive to publish research that increases buying and selling. A research report telling investors to just hold their shares does not make the bank money. In addition, this means the largest paying clients for research are those that trade the most; the hedge funds. This creates a further incentive for research to focus on the short-term. Therefore a key source of information and analysis in the market has a short-term bias, further increasing the short-term bias in company decisions. I return to this in Chapter 7.

Conclusion

In this chapter I have explained how the changes in the 1980s have led to a short-term focus. There is a mutually reinforcing cycle of short-termism between the different entities owning and controlling our companies. Management are paid based on the short-term share price performance. Share prices in turn have a short-term focus due to the short-term pressure on fund managers and research analysts.

This mutually reinforcing cycle is captured in a quote by Citigroup CEO Chuck Prince in 2007 just before the financial crisis began: "When the music stops, in terms of liquidity, things will be complicated. But as long as the music is playing, you've got to get up and dance. We're still dancing."[7] Chuck Prince knew there were longer-

---

[7] From an interview with *FT Japan* in July 2007.

term problems coming but felt compelled to maximise profit in the short-term.

This cycle is difficult to break, which partly explains why so many reforms have failed. This short-term focus is also responsible for the lack of investment highlighted in Chapter 1, which is accelerating the West's relative decline versus the East. The questions for the next few chapters are: What are the alternatives? How can we reduce the short-term bias?

Chapter Five

What are the Alternatives?

"Industry entirely left to itself, would soon fall to ruin, and a nation letting everything alone would commit suicide."
— Friedrich List (*Outlines of American Political Economy*, 1827)

So far I have told the story of company ownership and control in the UK and US, but what of the alternatives? How are companies in other countries owned and controlled? And are there bold new alternatives being proposed? These questions relate to the different ways that societies concentrate power in order to coordinate large scale activities.

Remember Chapter 2, companies were one step in the history of coordination. For thousands of years the main concentration of power in society was the ruler and associated wealthy elite. These concentrations of power enabled large activities to be coordinated. But most concentrations of power are eventually abused. Companies provided a whole new way to concentrate power in society, forming organisations with sufficient power to carry out a specific task. They provide an alternative

5. What are the Alternatives?

concentration of power to the state. As a result companies have enabled waves of investment from ocean trading to railways to the internet.

Companies have evolved differently in each country. Concentrating power in a slightly different way, taking a different balance between the need to coordinate large projects, against the risk that power is abused. As such each country has a different model for owning and controlling their companies. These characteristics lead to different balances between the short- and long-term, between the status quo and disruption. These differences in turn determine the direction our economies go.

In the US and UK, as described in the preceding chapters, we have a shareholder-centric model. Our companies are now run primarily for shareholder value. There are a large number of small shareholders, so that no one shareholder has much power. There is one board that is mainly made up of independent directors with no connections to management. Lastly there is little interference from the state. It is a very open, flexible and dynamic system. Companies can fail or be taken over. Management can be fired by their board and are held to account publicly by the stock market. However, the downside is that this has created a short-term bias.

What are the other models for company ownership and control? Can we learn from them? Do they enable a better balance between the short- and long-term?

Germany, Japan and South Korea

The German model, and in general across continental Europe, has much more concentrated ownership in companies. It is similar to the UK and US before the First

World War, except the large shareholders are not just families but are also other companies and banks. Related to this, Germany has fewer listed companies, as more companies are still privately held by a few large shareholders.

In Germany companies are more reliant on banks for finance than public capital markets. Rather than raising money by selling shares on the stock market, companies will generally seek a loan from a bank. It is then also common for a company's primary bank to hold a stake in the company. This developed after the Second World War, when companies were struggling for money so banks lent money but took stakes in the companies to provide security over the loan.

Another difference in Germany from the US and UK is cross-shareholdings between companies. Companies will often hold stakes in trading partners to cement commercial relationships. For example a consumer goods manufacturer might buy a small stake in a retail chain that sells its products. This creates an inter-locking web of companies within an industry. This produces longer-term relationships between trading partners, but is also more rigid as it is harder to change trading partners. This is in contrast to the UK and US where companies form commercial agreements with each other that can be broken relatively easily.

This ownership structure comes from a different view of business. Whereas the US and UK have been inspired by the famous economist Adam Smith to have free markets and competition, the German economic structure was influenced by the ideas of Friedrich List (1789–1846), who wrote that businesses should work together in the

5. What are the Alternatives?

nation's interest. Partly as a result of this, when Germany industrialised in the late 19th century companies were allowed to coordinate on prices. Companies could legally form cartels, the number of which increased from 4 in 1875 to 385 in 1905.[1] These cartels would cooperate in a number of areas and often have cross-shareholdings. This is the opposite of our modern system where any implication of collusion is met with a full investigation. This set the foundation for a much more collaborative structure for industry relations and company ownership than the UK and US.

In 1930s Germany the Nazis took this to the extreme, forcing small companies to merge together to form large companies dominating each industry. The state interfered strongly in business, instilling a view that the purpose of business was to serve the nation, not shareholders. Some historians called this "Listian economics gone mad". This extreme case shows us the difference in approach—are companies there to serve shareholders, the nation or society more broadly?

In recent years German company ownership has been drifting towards the US/UK model, but it still retains its differences. In 1998 German listed company ownership was: 10% banks, 13% investment firms, 14% insurers, 30% other companies, 17% individuals and 16% foreign.[2] Note the large holdings by banks and other companies, and the low holdings by individuals versus the US and UK, as shown in Chapter 3.

---

[1] Alfred Chandler (1990) *Scale and Scope*, Cambridge, Mass: Harvard University Press, 423.

[2] Caroline Fohlin (2005) "The History of Corporate Ownership and Control in Germany", *NBER* 2005.

Another key difference with the German model is that there is a two-tier board structure. There is a management board that manages the company. Then there is a supervisory board of which half is elected by shareholders and half by the employees, no management can sit on this board. This provides direct representation for employees in the ownership structure of companies. This has arguably meant that German companies have always taken a more balanced approach between the needs of shareholders and employees.

As a result of employee representation and the large shareholdings by banks and other companies, the power of shareholders and financial markets is much lower in Germany than the US and UK. It is argued that this enables German companies to take a longer-term view and encourages a fairer balance between employees and shareholders.

The downside is that the system is more rigid. Employee representation makes reorganising businesses more difficult, mainly in making it harder to fire people. The cross-shareholdings lock companies into commercial relationships, this makes it harder to change and hence for start-ups to gain ground. Management are also held to account by large shareholders, often in private conversations. Therefore while the German system may enable greater long-term investment, it does so at a cost of less flexibility and transparency.

The Japanese model is similar to the German model, partly because Japan modelled itself on Germany when it industrialised, both following the ideas of Friedrich List. Japan in some ways has taken the model one step further.

In Japan groups of companies form much tighter bonds between each other, connected by cross-shareholdings. Within each group there will generally be a bank and insurance company that will channel public savings into the businesses. These are called a *Keiretsu*. While ownership has been shifting towards the US/UK model, we still see a difference in the share ownership for Japan: in 2013 individuals owned 19% of Japanese listed companies, 21% by other companies, 21% by banks, 8% by other financial institutions and 31% by foreigners.[3]

The boards of directors are then made up of individuals from the other companies and banks within the *Keiretsu*. As such, outside shareholders in Japan have little influence. They can buy shares, but cannot hope to influence the decisions management make. Japan also takes the focus on companies serving the society one step further. Company management in Japan feel they have a strong duty to society. The purpose of companies is seen as serving the nation, preserving wages, providing stable employment and ensuring the success of other companies in the *Keiretsu*.

South Korea also has a similar structure for company ownership and control having modelled itself on Japan. It perhaps takes this further again; the Korean economy is dominated by large industrial groups called a *Chaebol*, similar to the Japanese *Keiretsu*. In 1995 the 30 largest *Chaebol* accounted for 41% of total domestic sales in South Korea.[4] There is also greater state involvement in South

---

[3] "2013 Shareownership Survey", Tokyo Stock Exchange.
[4] Barry Metzger, Bernard S. Black, Timothy O'Brien and Young Moo Shin (2001) "Corporate Governance in Korea at the Millennium: Enhancing International Competitiveness", *Journal of Corporation Law*, 26, 537–608.

Korea. The state helps coordinate business to ensure that investment is channelled into certain industries.

Partly as a result of this South Korea has been an incredible success story. Just before the Korean War in 1953 South Korea was poorer than the Philippines, with GDP per capita at 10% the level of the USA. Currently South Korea has an income level not far off the UK and around 70% of the USA's. South Korea now has successful global companies such as Samsung and Hyundai.

Similar to Germany the structure of company ownership and control in Japan and South Korea helps foster long-term relationships between companies and hence enables long-term investment. Companies are not influenced or controlled by financial markets, but instead by large controlling shareholders. These shareholders enable companies to invest longer-term.

During the 1970s and especially the 1980s the success of Japan and Germany led many to question the US/UK system of governance. The short-term focus of the 1980s take-over boom stood in stark contrast to the long-term relationships and higher investment levels in the Japanese and German system. US companies were increasingly losing out to German and Japanese rivals. Some people questioned if the US needed to model itself on Japan.

However, as the economic fortunes reversed in the 1990s so did the views on company ownership structures. The Japanese boom ended in the early 1990s and a two-decade economic hiatus set in. In contrast the US economy boomed in the 1990s. Further confirming the triumph of the US system was the collapse of the Soviet Union and East Asian financial crisis in 1997/8. All of this

5. What are the Alternatives?

helped to reinforce the dominance of the US/UK system of company ownership. The debate changed from whether the US should emulate Japan, to whether all company ownership systems would eventually converge to the US/UK model.

The US/UK model is seen as offering much greater flexibility than the German and Japanese system. Companies can fail and be replaced by new disruptive companies, such as the host of internet companies springing out of Silicon Valley. Industries can be realigned by mergers and acquisitions. Management can be incentivised to perform with share incentive schemes. New companies can raise finance more easily from public capital markets.

In contrast the model inspired by Friedrich List can be quite rigid, it is harder for companies to fail, and hence also harder for new companies to usurp the old. The Asian model in essence creates larger concentrations of power than we see in the US and UK. These concentrations can coordinate more long-term investment, but they are also more rigid and less accountable. Management of companies are held to account by large shareholders in private boardrooms, not through public trading on stock markets. This creates a more closed system for company ownership and control.

These structures for company ownership and control may enable greater long-term investment, but it does so at a cost; the system is more rigid and less accountable.

Large controlling shareholders

The ownership model in Germany and Japan suggests that we need large controlling shareholders to enable long-term action. Proponents of this model argue that to reduce short-termism we must solve the original principal-agent problem, highlighted by Adam Smith in 1776 and formalised by Berle and Means in 1932. The idea is that as long as companies are owned by hundreds of small passive shareholders, then decisions will be biased to the short-term by the mechanisms described in Chapter 4.

If shareholders have large stakes then they have more control over management and it is harder for them to sell. Selling a large stake is difficult, for as a shareholder sells this starts to push the share price down, the more they sell the more the share price falls. Hence large shareholders cannot sell their stakes quickly and therefore have an incentive to engage with management. This should then insulate companies from the short-term pressures of financial markets and enable long-term investment.

Proponents of this approach point to the longer view taken by Japanese, South Korean and German companies, as outlined above. We also see controlling shareholders taking a longer-term view with entrepreneur owners. Just think about the most innovative companies of the last few decades such as Microsoft, Google and Amazon. Most innovative tech companies are still controlled by their founders. Could these companies have taken the bets they did if they had to meet quarterly profit expectations?

Google is a prime example of a company that takes long-term bets, as the following example shows. In 2005 the US government agency DARPA held a competition for teams to design a driverless car. At the end of this people broadly concluded that this was a step too far for computers. Driving required too many variables and uncertainty to be handled by a computer. Not deterred by this Google decided to invest in solving the problem. The bet paid off and by 2012 they had clocked up 300,000 accident free miles. It is now just a matter of time before commercial adoption. It is hard to see a company beholden to financial markets able to make such a bet.

Masayoshi Son who I mentioned in the introduction is another example. To the disapproval of financial markets he acquired the mobile operator Softbank and invested heavily in mobile data. I once heard him give a talk where he explained with delight how financial markets had not believed his investment plans. How the share price had kept falling and financial analysts declared his investments unsound. His bet paid off, the return on the investments came through and the share price soared.

Fast growing industries such as technology are naturally dominated by entrepreneur owners as all the companies are quite young. In a similar way many fast growing emerging countries have a high proportion of companies owned by individuals. We see this in South Korea where the *Chaebols* are family controlled. We also see this in India where company insiders and their families own 45% of the value of all Indian companies.[5]

A number of Western commentators note the entrepreneurial drive this gives companies from emerging markets. Companies owned by one person are more prepared to make long-term bets, which often pay off. In

---

[5] Nandini Rajagopalan and Yan Zhang (2008) "Corporate Governance Reforms in China and India: Challenges and Opportunities", *Business Horizons*, 51, 55–64.

contrast Western companies influenced by stock markets seem cautious and overly focused on short-term profit.

In many ways the ideal owner of a business is a passionate and knowledgeable entrepreneur, someone who understands the intricacies of the business and has long-term horizons. The problem is all our businesses cannot be controlled by entrepreneurs. For entrepreneurs eventually die, ownership is passed to the family and eventually the family move on and no one is left in control.

This transfer in ownership is what happened in the UK and US. Companies were originally controlled by entrepreneurs, followed by their families and then when they sold out this led to hundreds of passive shareholders and professional management. The dominance of family controlled companies in emerging markets currently is in many ways similar to the US and UK in the late 19th and early 20th century.

Entrepreneur and then family control may enable long-term investment, but it is unlikely to last forever. Further to this it is not always desirable. As ownership passes to subsequent generations the magic of the original entrepreneur is often lost. It was after all under family control in the early 20th century that British businesses paid out near all their profits in dividends. Family owners wanted to support a certain way of life, rather than invest and grow the business.

Of course, no one is proposing that we return to family owned and controlled businesses. That would imply deep wealth inequality and concentrations of power in society with no means to hold them to account. However, there is a strong view that the US and UK needs to move towards larger shareholders with more control over management. The question which proponents of this view often ignore is; who are we transferring power to?

Simply transferring power to fund managers without changing incentives is unlikely to remove the short-term bias. Fund managers as outlined before have short-term incentives created by monthly performance assessment and yearly bonuses. If we create large shareholders that are in fact short-term focused fund managers, this is unlikely to replicate the long-term outlook of entrepreneur and family control. It also creates the question, how do we hold the fund managers to account? The principal-agent problem is simply moved one level up the ownership chain.

The problems this could cause are in some ways shown by private equity. Private equity works by a fund buying controlling stakes in a number of private companies. The fund will own them for around 5–8 years and then aim to sell them at a profit. This model has some benefits. It solves the principal-agent problem with controlling stakes and high incentives for management. The time horizon is also slightly longer than that of most listed companies. However, it creates extreme incentives for both private equity partners and management — it is in some ways the shareholder value focus on steroids. As a result private equity achieves great success at times and complete failure at others.

In the search for high returns private equity funds often cut costs aggressively to boost profits prior to selling. They often increase the level of debt substantially to enable higher cash pay-outs to themselves as shareholders. There are countless examples of companies forced into bankruptcy due to the high level of debt the private equity fund placed on the company. In the end there is still a short-term focus and in addition there is a significant reduction in accountability and transparency. The principal-agent problem is simply transferred up to the level of the private equity fund.

The problem of accountability is shown by the extremely high levels of pay in private equity. A fund will typically charge a 2% management fee and 20% of any increase in value. Therefore for a $10bn fund, if this increased by 50%, then the return is $5bn. 20% of this is $1bn to be split between the partners in the fund. If you want to get rich, work in private equity. I am not arguing against private equity, it performs a valuable function most of the time. But we would not want all our companies to be owned and controlled by a private equity type structure. The incentives are extreme and funds extract high fees.

I saw an example of the dangers of this while working as an equity analyst. An investment fund built a large stake in a European company. The fund then pressured the company to cut costs and return cash to shareholders. The company share price soared as it became the darling of the sector, the company to which all others were compared. The CEO was also revered, if only all CEO's could be like them. The fund manager who made the investment was also regarded as the most astute investor in the sector. However, after the CEO left, things started to fall apart. It turned out the company had been cutting costs too aggressively, not investing and sacrificing market share for short-term profit. The company eventually had to ask shareholders for more money and was acquired by another company. By this point the original fund had sold out making a tidy profit. This shows the risk of simply giving more power to fund managers without changing the incentives.

This risk is also shown further by the actions of the small but growing number of activist investment funds. These are investment funds that buy shares with the specific purpose of influencing management to increase the share price. There is a debate as to whether such activist funds improve the long-term performance of companies or not, but what is clear is that the primary aim of these activist funds is often to increase the amount of cash paid out to shareholders.[6] The activist funds look for a management decision that would lead to an immediate share price increase; this is often selling an asset or returning cash. This shows greater shareholder power without changing incentives risks reducing investment further.

Therefore simply shifting towards larger shareholders without changing the incentives for fund managers is unlikely to tackle short-termism. We would be transferring the principal-agent problem one step up the ownership chain and not necessarily solving the problem of short-termism.

Less power to shareholders

Another popular alternative to the current UK/US structure of company ownership and control argues quite the opposite; that we should reverse the 1980s and hence reduce the power shareholders have over management.

---

[6] "Shareholder activism and the implications for investors", JP Morgan, February 2014.

The argument is that many of the recent scandals have been caused by the shareholder value focus that began in the 1980s. Financial markets have a short-term focus and this is making our companies focus on quarterly profit. Proponents argue that companies should operate in the interests of all stakeholders, be they customers, employees or shareholders. Such "stakeholder capitalism" is in many ways similar to the "managerial capitalism" that existed in the 50s and 60s. It also has some similarities with Japan and Germany. It requires management or the board to balance the interests of the different stakeholders.

This argument has some appeal as financial markets do exert a short-term pressure on companies. However, while part of the diagnosis may be correct, the solution is not. Simply reducing shareholder power essentially puts our trust in management to make the right balance between the different stakeholders. It risks returning to a closed system of corporate governance similar to "managerial capitalism". It requires trusting in decisions made behind closed doors, with little ability to influence the outcome. It may remove the problems caused by excess corporate greed, but it risks removing the incentive to do anything at all.

Stakeholder capitalism would also be very difficult to implement. It is hard to see many companies voluntarily not acting in shareholders' interests. The change could be made legally, but shareholders and fund management groups are a powerful vested interest. It is hard to see them giving up the power they gained in the 1980s. Once the genie was let out of the bottle in the 1980s, it is hard to see it being put back in.

More important than these problems is that stakeholder capitalism misses the point; stakeholders' interests are only misaligned in the short-term. In the long-term the interests of most stakeholders in a company are aligned. In the short-term workers want high wages and company executives want low wages. But long-term both benefit from a successful company that can only be built on a careful balance of fair wages and sufficient profit margins to justify investment. Similarly, companies may wish to charge customers a high a price in the short-term, and customers want the opposite. But if companies charge too high a price the customers will eventually leave, or too low a price and the company may go bankrupt.

Therefore the complaints made by the proponents of stakeholder capitalism would be solved if companies took a longer-term view. There would be a more even and harmonious balance between the stakeholders if we extended the time horizons of all parties. We should focus on encouraging long-term thinking, rather than trying to shift power between stakeholder groups.

The trade-off between accountability and long-term incentives

All of the alternatives for company ownership and control are different ways to concentrate power in society. They all have good and bad points, with different degrees of long-term action, accountability and flexibility. As such it is very difficult to say if any one model is better than the others. This is because they are grappling with a problem inherent in all human coordination.

In many parts of human life we delegate power to someone to carry out a certain task. We give politicians the power to run the country, teachers to teach our children, CEOs to run businesses, doctors to keep us well. We can view all of these as principal-agent relationships. There is a principal who delegates a task to an agent.

The principal (voter, shareholder, parent) wants to ensure that the agent (politician, CEO, teacher) is doing a good job so they monitor what they are doing and maybe set some targets. The problem is that the agent understands what they are doing considerably better than the principal. CEOs know their business far better than shareholders. Politicians understand government more than the average voter. Parents cannot sit in a teacher's classroom all day. Hence there is a gap in understanding and information between the principal and agent.

Therefore if the principal wants to hold the agent to account, they must rely on a poorer understanding of the task than that held by the agent. Hence any short-term targets set by the principal will be a poor reflection of reality, and as such will invariably create skewed short-term incentives. Hence there is a choice, the principal either trusts the agent to carry out the task well, or puts in place short-term incentives that may have a perverse result.

In all delegations of power in society there is also a gap in information. As a result of this there is a choice between trusting that the power will be put to good use, versus relying on a poorer understanding of the world to hold them to account. We see this in a wide range of human activity, with a few examples below.

5. What are the Alternatives?

We send children to school to become productive future members of society. However, we want to incentivise teachers to do a good job therefore we set targets and performance pay based on exam results. As a result we have ever higher exam pass rates, but at the same time employers are claiming school leavers lack basic skills. The problem is that we skew the incentives of teachers to focus on the short-term outcome of exams, when in reality what we care about is how prepared our children are for life. In essence the drive for accountability has created a short-term focus to the detriment of children's education.

The same problem is seen in academia where there is an increasing use of targets. Professors and universities are set targets on how many academic papers they need to publish. This creates a bias away from those long-term risky research projects that might make a major breakthrough, in favour of shorter-term lower-risk projects. A number of prominent academics have spoken out against this. The physicist Peter Higgs, who in 1964 proposed the existence of the Higgs boson or often-called "God particle", said "It's difficult to imagine how I would ever have enough peace and quiet in the present sort of climate to do what I did in 1964". There is even a body in the US called the MacArthur Foundation fighting against this trend by offering grants for 5 years not attached to any targets or performance evaluation.

In all principal-agent relationships there is a balance between trust, enabling long-term action, versus accountability, leading to short-term incentives. We need some level of accountability and pressure to perform, otherwise our lazy side comes to the fore and not much is accomplished. But too much of this and we only act with the short-term in mind. If we rely on trust then this allows people to act long-term, but it means sometimes this trust will be abused and mistakes made.

This same trade-off applies to all the different models for owning and controlling companies. To concentrate power in society there has to be a delegation of power, for companies this is from savers and shareholders to management. Management know more about the business than the outsiders do. Therefore to hold them to account we need to rely on short-term observations that skew incentives to the short-term.

Some models for company ownership and control such as those inspired by Friedrich List rely more on trust, enabling long-term action but lacking in accountability. While others such as the US and UK hold management to account in an open and immediate way, but consequently create a short-term focus.

Conclusion

In this chapter we've seen how there are a wide variety of models and proposals for how we should own and control our companies. Essentially for how we should concentrate power in our society and hold it to account. None of these are perfect; all have varying degrees of long-term action, accountability and flexibility. This comes from a trade-off in all principal-agent relationships between accountability and long-term action. The US and UK system is very flexible, accountable and open, but as a result has a short-term focus. Many of the alternatives are less open and accountable, but do foster a longer-term approach.

5. What are the Alternatives?

What do we conclude? Is the US/UK system the same as Churchill said of democracy, the worst apart from all the others? Is a short-term focus the necessary cost of holding the concentrations of power in our society to account? We ideally want to keep the flexibility and openness of our current system, while fostering more long-term investment. Or is it possible to have the best of both worlds? This is the question for the next two chapters.

Chapter Six

Reforming Incentives

"All men having power ought to be distrusted to a certain degree." — James Madison, 4th US President (1787)

As should now be clear, the way our companies are owned and governed is a complex web of trade-offs. There is no perfect answer because we do not know the future and we cannot watch management the whole time. We need to concentrate power in society in order to coordinate large tasks, but we then face the question of how we hold that power to account? We want to incentivise management to perform, to monitor how they are doing, but we need to be careful not to create a short-term bias.

In the last chapter we saw how all systems have pros and cons. The system in the US and UK is the most flexible, innovative and open, but leads to a short-term bias. The systems inspired by Friedrich List foster longer-term investment but are more rigid and closed. We ideally want to keep the openness and flexibility, while fostering more long-term investment. The question for this chapter and the next is what reforms would achieve this?

The problem with current reforms is that they are generally a reaction to the last corporate scandal. Since the first companies hundreds of years ago there have been corporate scandals; management who have abused the power given to them to the detriment of employees, investors and the economy. Normally following each scandal there is public outrage and a series of reforms aimed at preventing the same scandal occurring again.

In the UK after the South Sea Bubble there was the Bubble Act in 1720 requiring new companies to be approved by Parliament. After the Wall Street crash of 1929 in the US was the Glass-Steagall Act that amongst other things separated commercial and investment banking. The excess of the 1980s take-over boom led to the Cadbury Code in the UK, which introduced separate audit committees and separated the role of CEO and Chairman.

Then in the USA following the dot-com scandals such as Enron was the Sarbanes-Oxley Act in 2002. This made misrepresenting financial statements a criminal offence. It also aimed to improve the independence of auditors by preventing a company's auditors also selling consultancy services. Following the recent financial crisis in 2007/8 the Dodd-Frank Act in 2010 introduced a shareholder vote on executive pay, greater disclosure on executive pay and a greater ability for shareholders to nominate directors to the board.

These reforms have slowly improved the governance of our companies and helped limit outright corporate fraud. However, this is quite different from reducing the short-term bias. Reforms too often seek to prevent the exact same crisis or scandal occurring again, but do little to tackle the underlying problem of short-termism. As if constantly fixing the leaks in a boat, without asking why does it keep leaking?

In Chapter 4 I explained how short-termism was caused by a mutually reinforcing cycle. Management pay is based on short-term share price movements. Share prices have a natural short-term focus, which is accentuated by short-term pressures on fund managers such as monthly performance assessment. This is further worsened by a pressure for research analysts in banks to write short-term focused research. All these factors compound on each other, increasing the short-term bias and making reforms difficult.

To reduce the current short-term bias we need to utilise this cycle in reverse. If we reform each element to have a longer-term focus this can compound in the opposite direction. Reforming one part of company ownership on its own, such as management pay, is unlikely to solve the problem. Instead we need to reform all parts of company ownership and control at the same time. This way a series of small reforms can have a magnified impact.

In this chapter I will run through a series of reforms that could help break this cycle of short-termism, primarily by focusing on extending the time horizons of management and shareholders. Then in the last chapter I will turn to an area of reform that is largely ignored, namely the research and analysis behind decisions.

1) Change in culture

Some commentators simply call on management to take a longer-term view, in the hope that some sort of epiphany will end the scourge of short-termism. They argue that a short-term focus is bad for business and therefore management should realise the error of their ways and act long-term. Such a shift in attitudes may be possible and would certainly be helpful but it is unlikely to be enough on its own.

Related to this hope that change can be achieved with no reforms are new regulations obligating fund managers to have a fiduciary duty towards the companies they invest in. The idea is that fund managers should not simply buy and sell shares, but should engage with management and support the long-term success of the businesses in which they are shareholders.

This may help shift attitudes modestly towards longer-term investing, but is unlikely to do more than this. This does nothing to reduce the short-term incentives on fund managers and therefore is unlikely to reverse the current decline in average holding periods. In addition a fiduciary duty will always be trumped by a fund manager's duty to deliver the best possible return for its clients. If this involves selling out at the first sign of trouble, then the fund manager will still sell out.

Further to this, fund managers still have little incentive to engage with management. Most fund managers hold small stakes in companies, therefore the cost of engaging with management is greater than any reward this might bring. If a fund manager disagrees with what management are doing, the rational decision remains to sell their shares rather than the costly process of trying to change management's decision. The risk is that new obligations on fiduciary duty will become another regulatory box-ticking exercise.

Attempts to shift the culture of management and investment are worthwhile and helpful. However, it is unlikely to be enough on its own. The problem of short-termism is caused by a powerful mutually reinforcing cycle; this will not be solved without reforms.

2) Board of directors

Another popular view is that reforming the board of directors is a key way to tackle short-termism. The board of directors is the group of directors elected by the shareholders at the AGM to run the company. Board directors have detailed knowledge of the company and the power to change management decisions. Therefore it appears a compelling place to start in tackling short-termism.

However, board members did little to stop the scandals and crises of the last few decades. Board members, no matter how independent they may be on paper, are often still strongly aligned with the CEO. The board of directors in many ways represents an advisory council for management, rather than a means to hold them to account. It also lacks transparency, no one knows if the directors are asking the right questions, or if they are being ignored. Further to this the board often responds just as much to the short-term pressure of financial markets as management.

There is also the risk that greater power to independent directors may reduce the ability of management to make decisions. The company may become run by committee rather than led by a CEO, decisions may be risk averse and made by a muddled consensus. As a result there is conflicting evidence on the value of greater power to independent directors.

6. Reforming Incentives

Some reforms to the board of directors may help, such as greater power to commission third party reports, or paying directors to work more days so that they are more engaged with the company. However, reforming the board is unlikely to make a significant difference to the cycle of short-termism.

3) Longer-term management compensation

What reforms would be more effective? As explained in Chapter 4 short-term management pay is a major cause of short-termism. This is already acknowledged as a problem and some reforms have been made; the problem is that these do not go far enough. There are broadly three ways to change executive pay; these are tax incentives, greater voting power for shareholders and disclosure. There is some role for all of these as outlined below.

One reform currently being introduced is greater voting power for shareholders on management pay. The UK and US recently introduced shareholder votes at the AGM on management pay. This provides shareholders with the means to demand changes in management compensation. An encouraging sign is that Fidelity, one of the world's largest fund managers, has begun to vote against pay deals that do not have at least a 5-year horizon. This reform could be strengthened by providing long-term shareholders with more votes on management pay, as these shareholders will value longer-term pay structures. This already exists for some companies in France and the EU has looked at adopting this.

Another reform is increased disclosure. If it is easier to see how management are being paid then investors will be more likely to call for reform. Disclosure is being improved but remains complex and unclear. As an analyst I once researched the pay schemes of 10 companies; it took a whole summer to finish the research, the disclosure looked comprehensive but there were serious gaps and definitions that could only be resolved by talking to the company. Few investors can dedicate such time to analysing the pay schemes of management; it is therefore difficult for them to apply pressure on such a topic.

Lastly, one of the most effective ways to encourage change is through tax incentives, which is not currently being used. Remember it was largely due to the tax system that share ownership transferred from individuals to institutional shareholders such as pension funds. Therefore the tax system can be an extremely powerful tool in reshaping corporate governance.

We could have a lower tax rate for compensation that is tied to long-term performance. For example the income tax rate for earnings over £500k could be 80% unless locked up in the company's shares for 10 years. Once someone is earning over £500k per year they cannot feasibly argue they need the money immediately, therefore it can be locked up in order to provide a long-term incentive.

A way to create even longer-term incentives is to adjust how pension investments are allocated. Company executives could be mandated to invest their pension fund contributions into the company, locked up until they retire. This would create an incentive for CEOs to not only invest for the long-term future of a company, but also to carefully plan succession so that the company will be well run after they leave. A good CEO should not only run a company well, but also build a strong team beneath them who can run the company after they leave.

Another popular idea is for senior management to invest in a company when they join. The majority of management buy very few shares in the company they run, instead gaining exposure to the share price by being allocated shares in a compensation scheme. The idea is that if management buy a long-term stake in a company they will act longer-term. They will be more like the ideal entrepreneur owners discussed in the last chapter. It has been proposed by some that this should be 10% of their wealth or equal to one year's salary.

Therefore there are a number of ways to encourage companies to adopt longer-term executive compensation. Some of these reforms are already being introduced, but we could and should do much more. These reforms are clear votes for shareholders on pay schemes, greater disclosure and tax incentives.

4) Longer-term investing

The next area of reform that would help break the cycle of short-termism is to encourage longer-term investing. Currently the short-term focus of financial markets puts a short-term pressure on company management. As stated earlier, the average holding period for UK stocks has fallen from 5 years in the 1960s to 7.5 months in 2007. This rapid trading of shares is a key contributing factor for short-termism. Ironically, rapid trading does not even lead to higher returns for investors. Most evidence shows that on average a buy-and-hold strategy outperforms active stock trading.

As a first step, similar tax incentives to management pay could be used to encourage fund manager compensation to be linked to the long-term performance of their fund. The tax system could discourage funds paying a bonus based on one year's performance. Tax incentives could encourage fund managers to invest a proportion of their wealth in the fund they manage, locked up until they stop working on the fund.

Another key way to lengthen investing time horizons is to use tax changes to encourage longer-term investing. The issue here is that penalising reforms need to be done globally, or business will just move elsewhere. For example a transaction tax sounds appealing by reducing the incentive for rapid trading, but evidence shows it just moves trading abroad. A second issue is that currently investment funds do not in general pay tax, instead individuals pay tax when they receive income from funds or when they sell their investment in the funds.

As a result of these difficulties effective reforms need to let people opt-in for a reward, rather than being penalised. Such reforms can be more effective as they are less likely to be resisted and do not create the incentive to be avoided. One example would be to create a new tax-efficient investment vehicle with a minimum average stock holding period of 3 years. This could attract funds from home and abroad and as such could form a significant part of the market. In the same way that tax benefits caused a flow of money into pension and mutual funds, the same could apply here.

The harder question is what tax benefits should such a vehicle have? Investment funds already do not pay income or capital gains tax. Therefore I propose a new corporation tax rebate. This sounds more difficult than it is. Firstly, corporation tax is already falling as it is becoming harder to enforce with increasingly globalised companies. As a result countries are slowly cutting corporation tax rates in a race to the bottom. Therefore we should get ahead of the curve and use reductions in corporation tax to incentivise the right behaviour.

The second point is that a corporation tax rebate would not be that difficult to implement and would be a crucial policy tool in the fight against short-termism. When a company fills in its tax return for the country in which it is listed, it can then calculate the amount of tax owed per share. Those shares held via these new investment vehicles would receive a proportion of this as a rebate. The remainder would be paid to the state as normal.

Related to this idea, minimum stock holding period requirements could be introduced for pension funds. Such a change could be phased in slowly so not to cause too much disruption. This would have a meaningful impact, but would only apply to investments by domestic pension funds in the home market. This would be 23% for the US, but only 5% for the UK.

Therefore just as tax benefits led to the growth of pension and mutual funds, tax incentives could move money into investment vehicles with a minimum average holding period. This could help shift the investment outlook of fund managers to the long-term. If fund managers had to invest on a 3-year view they would look for companies investing for the long-term, rather than only for companies that may announce a larger dividend or strong quarterly results.

Bringing it all together with an opt-in low tax regime

Lastly, the most powerful reform would be to combine all the reforms outlined above into a package of reforms that companies can sign up to in exchange for lower taxes. Again this would work on an opt-in basis to reduce disruption and resistance to change. This would effectively be a long-term focused corporate governance framework that companies would opt into in exchange for a lower rate of corporation tax.

Some potential requirements in the framework could be as follows: the CEO holding 10% of their personal wealth in the company's shares; longer-term based management pay; only report results annually rather than each quarter; increased votes at the AGM for long-term shareholders; increased time board members devote to the company; increased disclosure in certain areas.

This could even be formed as a new stock exchange. Companies could join the exchange by adhering to the requirements. Trading in shares could be restricted to certain time periods, rather than every day, for example shares could trade one day a week. There could even be a transaction fee on share trading with all proceeds being paid to the company. This would limit the incentive for short-term trading.

By offering tax incentives companies could choose to opt-in to such a regime by a shareholder vote at the AGM. If the benefits were made sufficiently attractive this could be an effective way to encourage change in how our companies are owned and controlled. Structuring reforms on an opt-in for rewards basis would make them far more effective than penalising reforms that are resisted and then subverted once introduced. Opt-in reforms are also far less disruptive to the status quo and therefore are less likely to lead to inadvertent damaging consequences. For example, a uniform transaction tax would simply move financial transactions abroad.

Companies opting in to such a regime should trade at a higher valuation; not only due to having a lower tax rate, but also as investors recognise the value in having a longer-term focus. Hence companies would want to join a new long-term focused framework, and investors would want companies they hold shares in to opt-in to such a regime.

Tackling short-termism is just like the classic prisoner's dilemma problem in economics. Everyone is better off if we all act longer-term, but as soon as some parties in the web of company ownership act short-term it also becomes in our interest to act short-term. We end up shifting from the optimal long-term equilibrium to the sub-optimal short-term equilibrium. Combining all the proposed reforms into a long-term focused corporate governance framework would enable the shift by all parties to a longer-term outlook.

Conclusion

The ownership and control of companies is a complex area with numerous trade-offs. This makes devising reforms that tackle short-termism difficult. In this chapter I have argued that reforms need to focus on tackling the mutually reinforcing cycle of short-termism outlined in Chapter 4. We need to shift the incentives of all the parties involved. This primarily involves creating long-term focused management pay and encouraging longer-term investing by fund managers. These two reforms already have some acknowledgement and some reforms have been made. The problem is current reforms are too modest, we need more effective reforms. Well-structured tax incentives are the most effective way of doing this. The most powerful means would be offering a new low-tax, long-term focused corporate governance regime that companies could opt into.

Chapter Seven

The Missing Piece

"Knowledge is power." — Francis Bacon (1597)

The reforms outlined in the last chapter would go a long way to tackling short-termism, but there is a missing piece in the puzzle. Debates around company ownership and control generally focus on where power lies and what the incentives are. I have so far argued that we should focus on extending the time horizons of all those involved. However, these debates largely ignore how and where the research and analysis behind decisions is conducted.

The debate on company ownership and control essentially boils down to how our companies can make better decisions. How can we create a structure of checks, balances and incentives that encourage the right decisions by management? The current debate ignores a key point, the decisions we take are only as good as the understanding of the world upon which they are based.

It is relatively easy to forecast the short-term future, but the further out we look the harder it becomes. Our ability to act for the long-term is only possible if we have an understanding of the future. If a company is to invest in a long-term project, it needs to know with some level of certainty that this will be successful. Similarly, if a fund manager is to buy a company's shares on a 5-year view, they need some good analysis to justify why the company will be worth more in 5 years. Good quality information and analysis is the foundation of good long-term decisions.

Further to this, the principal-agent problem that has plagued companies since they were formed stems from uncertainty about the future and an information gap between management and investors. It is because management have more information than investors that there is an incentive for them to artificially increase short-term profit. Most reforms battle with a trade-off between holding management to account with a short-term measure, versus trusting them to act in the interests of shareholders long-term. Closing the information gap and reducing uncertainty about the future enables longer-term action without any loss in accountability. It is the one reform not restricted by this trade-off.

As highlighted earlier, if share prices fully reflected the long-term implications of management action then there would be no problem with short-term stock-based compensation. This would create a perfect system where management were held immediately to account in a very transparent manner. There would in effect be no principal-agent problem. Therefore the closer we can get to this, the more that share prices can accurately reflect the future, the more we will move towards long-term decisions.

As an example, imagine if enough people had realised the flaws in the financial system prior to the 2007/8 financial crisis, perhaps it could have been averted? It was only long-term focused, in-depth research that would have uncovered the now well-known flaws in the system. A few people did but they were drowned out by the majority who did not. Improving the way we conduct research and analysis in financial markets should be a key way in enabling long-term action and averting another financial crisis.

The missing piece in tackling short-termism is reforming how we come to our understanding of the future. How is analysis and research conducted in financial markets? Would a different structure lead to an improved understanding of the world? And hence improved ability to make long-term decisions?

Cost of equities investing

Before going into the detail of how research is conducted in financial markets, there is another point that is largely ignored in debates on company ownership and control; this is the cost of share trading. Share trading may perform a vital function in holding management to account, but at what cost?

The fund management industry is in somewhat of a crisis. Fund management is the business of investing other people's money. For managing our money a fund typically charges 1% of the total value of the fund every year as a management fee. For example most of us pay someone to manage our pension savings for when we retire.

When fund management first started in the 1920s and 30s it was a very small proportion of the overall stock market. For the first time there were people who professionally traded shares on the stock market. It was therefore relatively easy to outperform the overall market as these early fund managers were competing against amateurs. People were therefore happy to pay a 1% management fee to gain such investment outperformance.

As the fund management industry grew it became much harder to outperform. As the charts on company ownership in Chapter 3 showed, professional fund managers have grown to now dominate our stock markets. Professional fund managers now compete against other professional fund managers. There is an arms race in gaining information and conducting analysis. Investment funds can no longer outperform the market for they have become the market. Worse than this, a number of studies show that investment funds underperform the market by their transaction costs. As a result people are less willing to pay a 1% management fee to gain in-line or below market performance.

The 1% annual management fee most active funds charge may not sound like much, but this equates to 15% of the annual profit of the underlying companies it invests in, or 25% of the dividends paid out to shareholders. This is because the average share price or company valuation is 15 times the annual profit, or 25 times annual dividends. Or, looking at it a different way, the average dividend yield is 4%. As a more tangible example I heard of a fund that managed $30bn, for this there was a team of 20 people. The fund only charged 0.75% per year, but this still equals $225m per year. Such fees are a significant cost for all our savings. Over the course of saving for your pension a 1% annual fee could reduce your final pension pot by around 30%. It is therefore no surprise that many investors are looking for lower cost alternatives.

In the quest to avoid management fees many investors are turning to passive investment funds. These are funds that buy a set basket of shares that form a certain index, for example the FTSE 100 or S&P 500. These funds do not make active investment decisions but instead automatically follow an index. As a result these funds charge very low management fees. These funds have grown as investors no longer want to pay the 1% management fee for active fund management. Passive funds now make up 17% of global mutual fund assets.[1]

The rise of passive funds not only presents a challenge for the investment industry, it changes fundamentally the role equities investing plays in the ownership and control of companies. The clue is in the name, passive funds represent the extreme case in fragmented passive shareholders, as no one is actively managing the investments that passive funds make in companies. The rise in passive funds risks substantially reducing engagement between shareholders and management. As we saw in Chapter 4, it is these slow shifts in company ownership that can build up to have profound impacts on the way our companies are run and decisions they take.

The rise in passive funds is not necessarily bad, there is a choice between a high-cost investment industry that plays an active role in company decisions, or we could have a low-cost industry where shareholders have limited influence on companies. When looking at how we own and control our companies we need to look at both

---

[1] Data from Lipper via "What Impact is the Growth of Passive Investing Having on IR?", *IR Magazine*, 31st October 2013.

the costs and benefits. Too often the debate ignores the cost side of this equation.

The fund management industry charges a hefty price for the role it performs in the ownership and control of companies. If management decisions are greatly improved by the share trading process then this is probably a price worth paying. Either way any reforms should aim to deliver the maximum benefit for the lowest cost to savers. Looking at both the cost and benefits of reforms has crucial implications for how and where analysis is conducted within financial markets.

How is analysis conducted currently?

Firstly, how is research and analysis currently carried out within the equities investment industry? As mentioned earlier, research on companies is carried out within investment funds and also by third parties that sell research to the investment funds. Most third-party research is carried out within investment banks, which is called sell-side research.

You may be wondering why do the investment funds not carry out their own research? The reason is that researching companies is a time consuming business, for which they do not have the resources. There are thousands of investment funds, each potentially investing in hundreds of companies. In contrast there are a much smaller number of third-party research providers. Producing company research requires scale; therefore a few banks run large research departments and sell this research to the hundreds of funds. The investment funds then use this research to decide which shares to buy and

7. The Missing Piece

sell. Only the very largest investment funds can justify employing large teams of in-house research analysts.

The benefits of scale within sell-side research means that an analyst will typically write research on just 10 companies. They may research these companies their whole career, seeing a number of CEOs come and go. The career path of a sell-side analyst is to become extremely specialised and knowledgeable about these companies and the sector they cover. Sell-side research departments have research teams organised by sector, such as banks, consumer goods, pharmaceuticals and transport. The largest banks then have research teams doing this all over the world.

In contrast, a fund manager has hundreds of stocks they could invest in. They will look at companies briefly to decide whether to buy and sell. If they own a stock in their fund they will follow it very closely, but as soon as they sell it, they will not. The research analysts at the large funds are still quite thinly spread, often covering in excess of 30 companies. Then in addition to this the career path of most people in investment funds is to become a generalist, this is in contrast to the specialist career path of the sell-side analysts.

Comparing the equities industry to politics, the CEOs are the politicians, the sell-side analysts are the press and the investment funds are the voters. No voter has the time to follow all the politicians around to see what they are doing, so the press do this. The voters then read the press and decide who to vote for. In the same way, no investment fund can do all the painstaking primary research on companies, therefore this is provided by the sell-side. The investment funds then use this, sometimes supplemented with their own research, and then decide which shares to buy. Hence there is a natural division of labour in how research is conducted.

Where should research be conducted?

This leads to the question, does research conducted inside investment funds or outside lead to a higher understanding of the world? What form of research would provide the information and analysis needed in order to take long-term decisions? What structure of research in financial markets would be more likely to foresee crises such as the credit-crunch? This may appear like a rather niche and unimportant question and as such it is largely ignored in the debates around equities investment. However, I argue this is a crucial question with important implications for our ability to act long-term.

Investment funds are seeking to gain an edge over their rivals, to help them outperform. Therefore any analysis they do will be kept strictly private. In contrast third-party research (i.e. sell-side) is made public, with analysis and conclusions shared openly, debated and built on by others. Third-party research therefore enables a higher level of analysis by enabling all those involved in equities investing to share and build on each other's analysis.

Secondly, third-party research creates a public debate around how companies and management are performing. It ensures management are held to account in a public forum, rather than behind closed doors. Companies are a key way we concentrate power in our society, it is better to hold them to account in an open

7. The Missing Piece

forum rather than in private meetings. Transparency is generally the best defence against abuses of power.

Lastly, third-party research helps create a level playing field between investment funds. Small investment funds cannot fund much of their own research and so rely on third-party research (currently sell-side research). This allows them to compete with the much larger funds that employ teams of in-house research analysts. This helps create a decent level of competition in the fund management industry. Without third-party research, the large investment funds would have a significant advantage, competition would be lower and so funds would be able to charge even higher management fees than the current 1%.

Therefore analysis conducted by third parties improves the overall quality of analysis in the market more than research conducted inside funds. It holds companies to account in an open forum. And it creates a level playing field between small and large funds, increasing competition and putting downwards pressure on annual management fees. When looked at in terms of the costs and benefits, public third-party research has a vital role to play in how we own and control our companies.

Returning to the analogy with democracy, imagine if there was no press, each voter would have to individually research what politicians were doing and saying. The overall understanding of the world which informed our votes would be much lower. The same is true in equities investment—if there is no third-party research we are effectively doing without the press. We are relying on private research carried out by each fund, with no sharing and public debate leading to an increased understanding of the world.

Problems with current third-party research

The problem is that the current form of third-party research is within investment banks. This creates numerous conflicts of interest and as a result there have been recurring scandals over the years. The most notorious were in the late 1990s tech-boom, which led to a $1.4bn fine for the major investment banks' manipulation of sell-side research.

The primary issue is that there is an incentive for investment banks to manipulate research to make money in other areas of the bank. Imagine what politicians would do if they were in control of the press? While regulations try to mitigate these conflicts of interest, biases still exist. One issue is that investment banks are paid for research when investment funds buy and sell shares, therefore there is an incentive for banks to write research that encourages trading. This creates a bias towards short-term focused research. Imagine if newspapers were only paid when you changed who you voted for?

Another problem with sell-side (third-party) research is that it is still too fragmented. There are too many research teams, with too few people on each team. There will often be at least 30 analysts writing research on each stock, but each analyst is stretched for time and so the research is of a lower quality than would be possible with more scale. The clients in investment funds frequently complain about multiple versions of the same low quality report. Imagine if there were 30 newspapers but each one

7. The Missing Piece

only had a few journalists, we would be stuck with 30 poor quality newspapers. This is the structure of sell-side research.

More scale per team would also allow for a greater variety of backgrounds. Currently most people working in sell-side research have a financial background. With larger teams there would be capacity to employ people who worked in the industry they research. The fact this does not already happen is probably a surprise to many. The people who write research on oil companies and ask the oil company CEOs questions will generally have never worked for an oil company. Increasing team size to incorporate people who have actually worked in industry could significantly improve the quality of analysis and information.

Therefore one reform to improve the quality of third-party research would be to enable consolidation. With greater scale per team there would be fewer reports, but each one would be of a higher quality. There would be less noise and more reasoned debate. As a stock analyst there are certain things that have to be done—run a financial model, comment on results and keep up to date with the news flow. Hence if an analyst is stretched for time it is the interesting in-depth analysis that gets sacrificed. It is this in-depth, more thought provoking analysis which is so critical to improving company decisions.

As a result of the recurring scandals, conflicts of interest and fragmented structure, many believe that sell-side research, and hence third-party research in general, is an unimportant part of company ownership and control. Some people believe that the system would be better off without sell-side research entirely. This is encapsulated in the UK government-commissioned Kay Review which said, "Looking forward, we see the sell-side analyst as a dispensable link in the chain of intermediation... Most asset management firms now undertake their own analysis and employ their own analysts".

This view ignores the significant benefit that third-party research delivers. In the analogy with democracy, the current approach would be as if following the phone-hacking scandal in the UK we had decided to do without the press entirely. Just because the current structure of third-party research has many problems, it does not mean having research conducted outside of investment funds is not important. We need to improve the provision of third-party research, rather than encouraging it to disappear.

This is more than just a niche area, it relates to how we concentrate power in our economies. It is publicly available information and analysis which holds power to account; this applies just as much with politicians as it does with companies. We can only act long-term if we have an understanding of the world that supports long-term action. Reforming how we conduct research in financial markets is a crucial way of achieving this.

How to improve third-party research

There is therefore an opportunity to significantly improve the provision of third-party research in financial markets. In doing this we would increase our collective understanding of the world and hence enable longer-term focused decisions.

7. The Missing Piece

The analysis so far points to three criteria for improving third-party research. Firstly, we need to remove the biases caused by third-party research currently being conducted by investment banks. Secondly, there needs to be consolidation to create more scale per team. And thirdly, research needs to be widely available to all investment funds in the market in order to create a level playing field and public debate.

There are a number of options for improving the structure of research in financial markets, from modest reforms to more radical. A simple first step is to enable consolidation of research providers. One reason for the fragmentation in sell-side research is that, within investment banking, research is in some ways a loss leader. An investment bank needs a research department in order to conduct other business such as company flotations and equity derivatives, hence banks choose to run sub-scale and stretched research floors in order to carry out these other activities.

A number of reforms could reduce the incentive for banks to run their own research floors and hence encourage consolidation through banks shutting down research, or merging research departments. One way to achieve this would be to require arm's-length communication between the research floor and trading floor, hence removing the benefit to investment banks from having their own research floor. Secondly, banks could be required to use an external provider of research in any investment banking business. These two reforms could help consolidation, creating the scale to produce higher quality research needed for long-term decisions.

Another reform is to change the way that research is paid for, removing the link to trading and investment banking, and hence removing the biases this introduces. Payment should instead be made directly for research. Funds could pay for research according to their assets under management rather than when they trade. Or funds could pay directly for access to different research services.

These reforms, however, struggle with a conflict between how research is paid for and meeting the three criteria highlighted above. Investment funds vary greatly in size and hence in their ability to pay for research. However, we also want equal access to research for all funds, to ensure a level playing field. How can research providers charge widely different amounts for access to research, while providing the same product?

This problem arises because publicly available research is what in economics is termed a "public good". It benefits everyone and costs nothing to be provided to an additional person, hence there is a risk that no one will pay for it at all. Investment funds only want to pay for research that will help them outperform their competitor funds. They have little interest in funding research that improves the understanding of everyone in the market; they want to pay for an advantage. This conclusion leads to a more radical reform for improving research in financial markets.

Investment funds could pay a research levy according to their size. This money would then be used to pay for research that would be available to everyone for free. There could be five independent research houses that would be paid by such a levy. The money could be

7. The Missing Piece

allocated by a mixture of votes by investment funds and readership statistics. Some of the allocation could also go on long-term research, or topics such as executive pay.

These new research houses would have greater scale than current sell-side research teams. With this scale they could focus on producing the painstaking primary research that is only possible with a large research team and sufficient time. Payment would not be linked to trading or investment banking. And lastly the research would be publicly available to all investment funds as well as the general public.

This need not be that disruptive to the existing structure. Existing sell-side research teams could build off the free research from the independent research houses. Investment banks may even welcome this as a way to reduce costs, as they would no longer need to employ such large research teams.

The cost of such a research levy need not be that high and certainly significantly less than other parts of the equities investment chain charge. For example, the total fees auditors charged companies in the FTSE 350 for checking their accounts was £669m in 2012.[2] Or the total market capitalisation of UK companies is £2.5tn – if only half of this is run by funds charging 1%, then the total fees collected by fund managers is £12.5bn each year. The cost of a levy could be significantly less than this.

Therefore a number of reforms could improve the provision research in financial markets, from modest reforms enabling the consolidation of research floors between investment banks, to changing the payment mechanism to a research levy enabling large independent

---

[2] "Auditing the Auditors", Financial Director audit survey, 2012.

research houses to form. There is not space here to go into the exact details on how each of these options would work. The important point is that improving the quality of external research is possible and it is vitally important to enabling longer-term decisions.

Towards a new structure of company ownership

The provision of high-quality research for free would not just help longer-term decisions it would also help create a new structure of company ownership. We currently have a structure where investment funds compete with each other in a game with no winners. They all claim to have a proprietary investment method that gives them an edge over rivals. To pay for this they charge 1% annual management fees. As a result we have a high-cost investment industry that places a drag on our savings and pressures companies into making short-term decisions.

The answer is to stop expecting the impossible. To stop expecting all investment funds to outperform, and alongside this to stop paying investment funds such high fees in the expectation they will outperform. With the reforms proposed in this book we can move away from the idea that all investment funds should outperform. We can move towards a structure for company ownership with lower annual management fees, a longer-term outlook and one where decisions are based on a higher overall understanding of the world.

Instead of shifting money to passive funds, money could move to funds that only charge 0.25% per year and rely heavily on free publicly available research. Such low-cost funds would sit between current active and passive funds, taking active investment decisions, but holding investments for much longer periods of time, charging lower fees and running with a lower cost structure. These funds would neither claim to have a proprietary investment method or to be able to consistently outperform.

This also ties into the idea of a tax efficient investment vehicle with minimum average holding periods, outlined in Chapter 6. New tax efficient longer-term focused funds would be perfectly placed to charge a lower annual management fee. The long-term corporate governance framework would also help this transition as longer-term investors would support companies moving to a longer-term focused governance framework.

As shown in Chapter 3 and 4, it is small changes in company ownership that build up over time that can have profound impacts on how companies are run and the decisions they take. Seemingly small changes such as how research is conducted in financial markets can build up to have a significant impact on how decisions are taken in our economy.

Conclusion

The current debate on company ownership and control wrongly ignores how analysis and research is carried out. The principal-agent problem that has plagued companies since their inception is founded on uncertainty about the future and an information gap between management and shareholders; this can only be overcome with good quality research. The ability to act long-term is founded on an understanding of the future, which is in turn founded on research. The quality of our decisions is only as good as the information upon which they are based.

The missing piece in tackling short-termism is improving our understanding of the world. In this chapter I have made the case that research and analysis is better conducted outside of investment funds. This enables greater scale per team, sharing research in a public debate, holding management to account in an open process and creating a level playing field between investment funds. This last point is important because currently fund management charges a high fee for managing our money.

There are a number of ways that third-party research could be improved, from encouraging banks to merge research floors to an industry wide research levy. The main point is that regulation needs to acknowledge the important role the third-party research provides.

Not only is better information and research critical to acting longer-term, but the best way to hold power to account is with transparency and information. Our democracy would be nothing without a free press. Likewise a shareholder democracy needs publicly available information and analysis.

Chapter Eight

Conclusion

We all know about the rise of the East and how China will probably become the world's next superpower. Many see this simply as the result of a large population and low wages catching up with our own. These factors are important, but they miss a crucial development; the rise of the East is also down to higher investment levels. China is already taking the lead in a number of high-tech industries, just as Japan and South Korea did before. This is partly due to much higher capital and R&D investment. In the West we must increase investment or our decline will accelerate.

In the West our primary means of investment is through large listed companies. Companies formed for this very purpose 150 years ago, acting as a concentration of capital that can coordinate activity and investment in large-scale projects. The problem is that our companies have developed an increasingly short-term focus. Companies focus on short-term profit and cash returns in order to justify ever increasing executive compensation, at the expense of long-term investment. This problem is becoming increasingly acknowledged, but the reforms remain inadequate. Reforms are often knee-jerk reactions following a crisis. Reforms may prevent the exact same crisis happening again, but do not tackle the underlying problem.

The cause of short-termism relates to the same challenge which has plagued companies since their inception, which is the principal-agent problem. How can shareholders ensure that management act in their interests? The solution to this creates a trade-off between accountability and long-term action. To hold management to account we must invariably rely on short-term observations that create a short-term bias. This means that most reforms must be a compromise.

Many proposed reforms simply move power between different groups, whether that is shareholders, fund managers, management or board directors. I argued these are unlikely to solve short-termism. Instead we need to extend the time horizons of all those involved. We can do this with tax incentives to encourage longer-term compensation and investment. Creating a new opt-in long-term focused governance framework would be a powerful means of achieving this.

In addition to this we need to improve the quality of research in financial markets. Decisions are only as good as the information and analysis upon which they are based. This would also create a level playing field between investment funds, increasing competition and so reducing fees that slowly eat away at our savings.

Many argue that the solution to short-termism is to return to a more closed system of company ownership, that we need to return to controlling shareholders as we had before the First World War and as currently exist in Asia or fast growing tech industries. Or that we need to remove the influence of financial markets all together and

8. Conclusion

put our trust in management and the board. However, I argue that we can keep the transparency of our current system while still fostering long-term investment. We just need to lengthen the incentives for all those involved and improve the quality of analysis upon which decisions are made.

Reforms to encourage companies to invest long-term again is one of the most important issues of our time. Without such investment our economies in the West cannot hold their own against those of the East. We should worry less about what our politicians are doing, and instead focus on getting our companies investing again. Once this is done we can return to worrying about how to share the wealth our companies create.